Rachel,
you are [...]
to the house [...] [...]
Continue to persevere and to
stir the gifts He has
given you.
Love,
Barbara Joyce Brooks

Hannah and Her Sisters

Hannah and Her Sisters

A Call for Women in the Church to Love As Jesus Loved

Revised Edition

Barbara J. Brooks

Publisher's Cataloging-in-Publication Data

Brooks, Barbara Joyce, 1954-

    Hannah and her sisters : a call for women in the church to love as Jesus loved / Barbara J. Brooks.— Revised ed.

        p. cm.
    Includes bibliographic references.
    ISBN 978-1-312-31432-0 (revised ed.)
    ISBN 978-1-312-39371-4 (academic ed.)

Examines the often tense relationships between women in the church. Helpful to those who need encouragement on either side of the issue of emotional wounding that sometimes occurs in church, as well as the leaders who may be called upon to help both victims and offenders find healing and forgiveness.

    1. Interpersonal conflict—Religious aspects— Christianity. 2. Christian women—Church.
3. Interpersonal conflict—Church—Emotional wounding.
4. Interpersonal relations—Religious aspects—Church.
I. Brooks, Barbara Joyce. II. Title.

    BV 4527. B 2014
    248—dc22

Contents

Preface

Hannah and Her Sisters is one story with many characters and many experiences. It is based on the biblical character Hannah, whose story represents all women in the church who have been emotionally wounded in a manner such as that which is described in these pages. Hannah's sisters are other women who also have a relationship with Christ. While my focus is on church relationships, these sisters are not always the women with whom she regularly serves. They are sometimes women she works with, is a neighbor to, or even relatives. These women, out of their own pain, ignorance, thoughtlessness, or many other conscious and unconscious motives, cause Hannah pain, tears, and turmoil that often spill over into other relationships and cause disharmony and division. Hannah and her sisters are unified by the blood of Christ and the indwelling Holy Spirit. They are all flawed, yet loved by our Savior—and we hope, by one another.

This book is not meant to merely criticize and find fault with women in the church. It is my heartfelt belief that Christian women are the most loving, supportive, kind-hearted sort to be found anywhere. Neither is it meant to simply vent about petty mistreatment that we need to just "get over." I suffered a great deal of anxiety as I wrestled with my concern that there would be those, especially outside of the church, who might read it and conclude that we are argumentative, immature, and touchy. I struggled with whether or not the book should be written at all. Should I air our dirty laundry and hold us up to additional criticism? But within the church the issue discussed here is no secret, and many women are hurt, angry, and even divided in fellowship because of it. I believe that we have the power to change.

I should also add that *Hannah and Her Sisters* is not meant to be therapeutic; you will not find "steps" to changing or healing. I am not a professional counselor, therapist, or psychologist. I am a minister, I have hurt and been hurt, and I am called to walk beside other hurting women with the wisdom and insight that God, for His own secret purposes, has given me. I will recommend resources for those who are seeking therapeutic care, but my purpose here is to share observations, advise, and encourage change. I believe that bringing attention to this issue and calling for personal accountability is a major step toward healing. That is my purpose for writing.

Women bear a unique kind of pain. (Yes, I know that men most certainly do, too, and I am one of the greatest champions of *their* needs and *their* unique gifting to minister to *their* pain.) As women, we need to minister to one another's pain and needs, and we need to celebrate one another's joys and victories. Thus, I felt that I *must* write this book. Christ not only wants His bride, the church, to come to maturity (Ephesians 4:11-16), but He has also commanded us to *really* love one another (John 13:34). Mine is but one small voice raised in the struggle.

Acknowledgements

There have been so many men and women who have touched my life in such a special way, that I cannot list them all. If I omit any of you, please forgive me.

My mother, Joyce Agnes Brooks, sacrificed so much in rearing me, which made the writing of this book possible intellectually and spiritually. You are my heart, Mom, and as your adult child, I am grateful for your loving care. You have endured great pain, both physically and emotionally, and I am eternally grateful for your sacrifices for me. What you have done in and for me has reached into the Kingdom of God. My sister, Cynthia L. Tyler, is so deeply a part of me that my imagination has no room for a "me" without her. I love you so much, Cyn. You are more than my big sister, and you are stronger than you know.

Among the very special women with whom I regularly fellowship, I am especially grateful for Nancy Compton and Shelda Clinkscales. Nancy, you are a gem. You are my friend and the epitome of what a pastor's wife should be. Shelda, women need friends like you, who make it all right for us to be ourselves, while inspiring us to be even better. All of the women of Hope Bible Fellowship Church have touched me in a special way. Thank you for what you have given me.

My pastor, Rev. Jimmie D. Compton, Jr., is a wonderful example of Christian manhood. Never have I met anyone who supports the gifts and passions and dreams of others as you do. Your intellect, work ethic, love for others, and love for Christ inspire me in immeasurable ways. Thanks for supporting and encouraging me in so many ways to make the writing of this book possible.

I honor my late grandmother Elizabeth Johnson, who was a pastor's wife, with this book. Grandma knew these and many struggles. She was the strength of Christian womanhood who inspired me to want "more Jesus." She lived for the love of Christ. I would do well to love as she did: from "Way down in my old sanctified soul!"

Many close family members have been so dear to me throughout my life. Aunt Bobbie and Uncle Emanuel, you are more than special.

To my nephew, Paul "Nick" Tyler: I hope that you will *always* embrace the depth and the breadth of Jesus' love for you. He has great value for you, and so do I. You are fearfully and wonderfully made. I love you with all of the love that I would have poured out on my own child. My prayer for you is that you will encounter God in a personal way and forever walk in His love.

There were thirteen people who told me that what I would say here was important. Your support validates this work in ways that you will never know: Dr. Donna Thomas of Ashland Theological Seminary, who supported and affirmed the concept of this book as an academic effort; Cyn, Kathy, Carol, Robyn, Naomi, Nancy, Carolyn, Tamra, Sheila, Darlene, Tanyau, and Madiene; God knows your hearts, and He knows my love for you all. Thank you.

Above all things and above all matters, I give glory, honor, and praise for this book to my Lord and Savior Jesus Christ. From the seed through its many revisions, my purpose has been nothing more than to bring glory to Him and positive change to the church. As He has purposed it, so will it be.

Chapter 1

Hannah

1 Samuel 1:1-8

There was a certain man from Ramathaim, a Zuphite from the hill country of Ephraim, whose name was Elkanah son of Jeroham, the son of Elihu, the son of Tohu, the son of Zuph, an Ephraimite.
2 He had two wives; one was called Hannah and the other Peninnah. Peninnah had children, but Hannah had none.
3 Year after year this man went up from his town to worship and sacrifice to the LORD Almighty at Shiloh, where Hophni and Phinehas, the two sons of Eli, were priests of the LORD.
4 Whenever the day came for Elkanah to sacrifice, he would give portions of the meat to his wife Peninnah and to all her sons and daughters.
5 But to Hannah he gave a double portion because he loved her, and the LORD had closed her womb.
6 And because the LORD had closed her womb, her rival kept provoking her in order to irritate her.
7 This went on year after year. Whenever Hannah went up to the house of the LORD, her rival provoked her till she wept and would not eat.
8 Elkanah her husband would say to her, "Hannah, why are you weeping? Why don't you eat? Why are you downhearted? Don't I mean more to you than ten sons?"

This was Hannah. In our twenty-first century world, women who choose not to marry or have children remain a minority, but they are not normally treated as outcasts. Their choice may not be widely popular, but it is generally respected by others. For reasons that I need not go into here, that choice is less popular in the church than in the world, but it is not as uncommon as it once was. This option did not exist in the ancient times in which Hannah lived. To illustrate her agony more clearly, please allow me to briefly take you out of our modern culture and give you some Old Testament background.

The very first command God uttered was, "Be fruitful and increase in number . . ." (Genesis 1:28). Every married couple took this command seriously. Children were the goal of their marriage as a guarantee that the husband's family line would continue. God's promise to Abraham was that he would be the father of many nations. Children were viewed as proof of God's favor and blessing; barrenness was viewed as a curse (Genesis 30:23; Exodus 23:26).

To the Hebrew people (Israelites as we now call them), who had a unique relationship with God, childlessness was evidence that one was separated from Him because of sin. Moreover, it was almost always the wife who was held responsible for a couple's childlessness. Although there are many places in Scripture where the matter of barrenness is raised, men are only directly associated with it in one of those instances (Deuteronomy 7:14). Polygamy was often the means by which heirs were guaranteed. Hannah bore her shame alone not only because Elkanah had fathered children with Peninnah, but because of the cultural standards that already held her responsible.

Hannah was not complaining because some trivial whim did not go the way she had hoped. Her pain was understandable. The one closest to her repeatedly failed to sympathize with the agony that was so deeply rooted in her heart. The phrase, "her husband would say to her . . ." (v. 8) indicates that this scenario was not new. Surely Elkanah's words threw salt into Hannah's already existing wound, and then opened a new wound altogether.

But let us not lose sight of the immediate cause of Hannah's pain. If she had been the only wife of a loving husband whose view of his role in her life was that he alone fulfilled her deepest desires, would she still have been in pain regarding her barrenness? Certainly. Especially in the unforgiving times in which she lived. But to the extent that we read here? Probably not. Surely her husband's undivided love and attention would have offered her some consolation, even if it were minimal.

Peninnah provoked and irritated Hannah because of a condition that Hannah neither chose nor controlled. The effect on Hannah was complete, and it was consistent with the horror of barrenness in her time. She was depressed and disgraced because of how her condition was viewed in her culture and because of her own unfulfilled desire.

Hannah had been spitefully treated by Peninnah, and as a result, she was emotionally wounded. If we can bring her from the desert of her time to the modern church, we will find that she represents women in churches today who endure mistreatment from other women in church—their sisters in Christ—and become, like Hannah, wounded. Whether the words, behavior, and attitudes that lead to her woundedness are intentional or not, these present-day Hannahs are on the receiving end of unloving, un-Christlike behavior from present-day Peninnahs. This is unbecoming to believers in Christ.

In the modern church setting, Hannah's pain is often cloaked in her silence and Peninnah's denial. The jabs she endures are subtle at times, but at other times they are painfully clear. Whether we fully appreciate her predicament or not, we can probably relate to the frustration she feels and recognize the type of emotional wounding she must bear at Peninnah's hands.

Hannah also had a concern that was much greater than Peninnah's agitation. Her barrenness brought her indescribable pain, and the biblical account goes on to teach us many lessons from the way she dealt with that burden. Scripture portrays godly women with greater concerns than hurt feelings from the beginning of time. Still, God cares about issues of emotional wounding like this one, and He wants us to be mindful of those "little foxes that ruin the vineyards" that He warns us about (Song of Songs 2:15). Therefore, the Holy Spirit inspired the author of 1 Samuel to leave this account of the tears Hannah shed for her greater concern—her barrenness—and also for the emotional wound inflicted by Peninnah.

We owe our Hannahs more than whispers and gossip and our complaining with others about how ashamed of herself Peninnah should be. Hannah's pain matters. The pain that you and I and our sisters in Christ have endured matters. Our healing begins with and must be continuously covered with prayer.

> *Father, I lift up the heart of every woman who is reading this book who has been hurt in any way by her sister in Christ. I thank You that You love her in a way that none of us can comprehend, and that Your love reaches into every area of her life. You are concerned about her pain, and You would have her to prosper and be whole as*

she serves You. I pray that she will seek You, and that Your will for her relationship with those who have wounded her would prevail. I come against every plot of Satan to accuse her, to encourage her to seek revenge, or to cause her to respond in any way that is not pleasing to You. I rebuke the lies that have been uttered and the lies she has believed. Help her to remember the cross! Even in her pain and anger, help her remember that You died for her to be free and victorious! In the Name of Your Son Jesus Christ. Amen.

Chapter 2 Peninnah

Polygamy was very common in ancient times, even though Scripture clearly indicates that it was not God's will (Genesis 2:24). Once God's original plan for humanity was violated in the Garden of Eden, the door opened for sin, including the abuse of women. If a woman was unmarried, she often had no means of support other than prostitution or selling herself into slavery. Unfortunately, polygamy became one of man's twisted means of stepping in with his own plan when God's will has been transgressed.

The Hebrew word for the second wife means "rival," just as it is stated in verse 6. It is clear that there was bitterness and jealousy between the polygamous wives—that was the nature of that Old Testament beast. A *rival* is one who competes with another for the same object. According to the definition, understanding, and expectations for the role, there would not likely be peace between them.

There have been times that we have all made an insensitive comment that hurt another person without our having had any intention of doing so. For example, a church member might go on and on about her husband having turned down a job, without knowing that she is being overheard by a woman whose family gets by on welfare because she has been unemployed for several months. On the other hand, that same sister might have been well aware of that person's circumstances but convinced herself that she should wait for the less fortunate woman to be within earshot in order to share in her "good news."

An acquaintance recently shared with me how offended she was after having received hurtful treatment from a woman in her church about what she thought was an insignificant issue. She asked me over and over, "Do they know what they are doing? Do they *know*?"

Examine your heart. If you know that you have hurt a sister—intentionally or not—you should lose no time in offering your sincere, heartfelt apology. We sometimes know the effects of our words or behavior, and sometimes we do not. But in our hearts, which we often call "the back of my mind," the Holy Spirit convicts us without our permission. Our hearts cannot deny intentional sniping, even if our minds are too stubborn or we are too ashamed of our own behavior to admit it to ourselves.

I struggled with whether or not the extent of Hannah's pain was what Peninnah intended. But there is no arguing with what the text clearly states. The passage tells us that it was at Peninnah's *repeated* and *intentional* agitation ("kept provoking her . . . in order to," v. 6) that Hannah became depressed and was driven to tears. There is no room for us to doubt Peninnah's intentions. "In order to irritate her" means exactly that. Whether Peninnah's darts are subtle or more obvious, we are dealing with women who intentionally cut their victims with their words and actions.

~

In a doctoral level seminary class in transformational leadership, I was participating in an exercise designed to illustrate the difficulty of one leader in a congregation attempting to solve every problem or issue alone. It was a "tag— you're it" kind of game. One person started out as "It," and when she tagged one of the runners (the other members of the class, who represented the problems), they then became a growing team and worked together to tag those runners. The It team grew larger as the number of runners became smaller, making it much easier to corner and tag the dwindling group of problems.

As the instructors explained the process, a woman who was there as a church leader but not a seminary student volunteered to be It. Then, just as the game began she said to me, "I'll start with you."

"Why?" I asked her. I was smiling and good-natured, pretending to be nonchalant despite my discomfort with having to be so physically active in a public setting. I was trying to force myself to be okay with playing the game.

"You're an easy target," she responded.

I weighed over two hundred pounds. *Shut up, Peninnah!* She had planned to attack me with her words just as she did with her game strategy. The humiliation washed over me like a flood. From years of teaching teenagers who are often so openly vicious with their comments, to the snide smirks of adults in settings of every type, I knew that the taunting and mockery that brutalized me in my childhood had not been left there. I knew that I was being naïve, but I had tried to convince myself that the abuse could not follow me into settings with mature church leaders who taught others the biblical principles of love and unity. The reality was quite jarring.

When I talk about accountability in Chapter 5, remember this incident. Although I want you to be careful about the "tapes" you allow to play in your head, you will no doubt recall some of your own painful encounters with women who were insensitive, thoughtless, or mean. My point here is that there are times that we all—and I think we know when—need to shut up.

Now I want to ask you to put yourselves in Peninnah's shoes for just a minute. This book would have no purpose if I were to suggest that her behavior always be ignored or excused. "Get over it" might have some merit in some circumstances, but it is a cold, unloving, and presumptuous attitude to take toward someone who is understandably in pain. Still, in order for the Hannahs to heal, it might help them to attempt to understand the Peninnahs.

We have different social and cultural values and have come through several thousand years of "sophistication," but the hearts of women have not changed. God is not wiring us any differently from how women were wired three thousand years ago in terms of our emotional needs—the needs of our hearts.

Imagine being a second wife and knowing that your husband loved his first wife more than he loves you. Elkanah had married Peninnah only to fulfill his desire for heirs, and that would have been clear to Peninnah. After verse 4, where Elkanah dutifully but unlovingly provides for Peninnah, her name is never again mentioned in Scripture. Her identity or personhood was consumed in her role, "rival," and that role defined who she was.

Peninnah had been brought into the household of a wealthy and godly man. Her role was to provide him with heirs. Given the culture in which she lived, she would have been aware of the status of women like herself who served this purpose. However, we do not need to try to guess as to how she should have *expected* to be treated; her reality was that she was slighted year after year (vv. 3-5). This feast was only one of many instances in which Elkanah attempted to make Hannah feel better at her expense. Peninnah had reason enough to be unhappy, and her unhappiness found a weaker victim.

Have you ever known a woman who was married only to be a breeder? Years ago I knew a man who desperately wanted children. At that time, he was single and in his late forties. His true love was a woman closer to his own age and social status who wanted to be neither a wife nor a mother. He married a much younger woman who did not know how to be a wife because she was a child herself, still in her teens.

Under the pretense of disgust with her inadequacies as a wife and the mother of his child, he abused her emotionally, physically, and verbally, while continuing to enjoy the company and affection of the woman he truly loved. He was able to manipulate and frighten his wife and take advantage of her immaturity. With far greater financial and intellectual resources than she possessed, he managed to take their child and raise him as a single parent.

This man's despicable behavior went far beyond what I am describing here concerning the Old Testament motive for polygamy, but the point is, he desired his young wife only as a breeder, and it was not long before she realized that. This type of scenario does not happen frequently, but again: *Put yourself in Peninnah's shoes.*

Peninnah aimed at and hit her target every time she provoked Hannah to tears. She was hurt, so, powerless to hurt Elkanah, she struck out at the only other individual on whom she could inflict pain. That would be Hannah.

Over the past few years, a saying which you have probably heard has become very popular: "Hurt people hurt people." This sounds so simplistic, almost trite, but it is very true. In the book of the same title from which that saying was taken, the author, Dr. Sandra Wilson, explores the notion that all of us have been hurt and in turn, hurt others, intentionally or not.[1]

I cannot identify every possible motive for Peninnah's behavior. Maybe your Peninnah has been victimized herself. There is also the possibility that she is simply petty or immature or

---

1. Sandra Wilson, *Hurt People Hurt People: Hope and Healing for Yourself and Your Relationships* (Grand Rapids, MI: Discovery House Publishers, 2001).

mean-spirited. Unfortunately, that latter type does exist, even in the church.

Regardless of her motive, God's will for His people is unity. Consider this admonition to the church in Ephesians 4:

> 1 As a prisoner for the Lord, then, I urge you to live a life worthy of the calling you have received.
> 2 Be completely humble and gentle; be patient, bearing with one another in love.
> 3 Make every effort to keep the unity of the Spirit through the bond of peace.

Though gently worded, this is a stern warning for all of us. It is no less true for the emotionally wounded Hannahs than it is for the Peninnahs with their verbal daggers and darts. We are all obligated to humble ourselves and strive for unity. Even as we dodge those daggers, we are not excused when we come up cursing and tossing them back. God wants us to love Peninnah just as He does. This requires that we make every effort to make these relationships right—not just clean them up on the outside with faking and denial.

The Hannahs who are reading this are quite likely to be hurt and angry about the way they have been treated. Although your anger is justified, Hannah, it is for your own sake that you allow God to heal you. Peninnah's behavior should not be excused, but she needs to be understood. She is a guilty victim. We must acknowledge both aspects of her behavior.

Most of you are probably familiar with another popular saying, "He looked beyond my faults and saw my needs." What a blessing of grace this is! Those exact words are not found in Scripture, but that is the meaning of one of the best understood sayings from the cross: "Father, forgive them, for they do not know what they are doing" (Luke 23:34). This is the scriptural basis of the "hurt people" theory. Jesus looked beyond the actions of those who had mocked, scorned, and viciously beaten Him and saw that they needed salvation, understanding, and a change of heart.

The Peninnahs among us need all of those. They are likely already saved (although we cannot assume that just because they are church members). But they certainly need understanding and a change of heart. Only the Holy Spirit can accomplish the dual work of penetrating the stony places in Peninnah's heart and helping Hannah understand her.

I would like to lead you in prayer for your Peninnah. I ask you, if you are so moved, to fill in the blanks concerning your personal situation, or to stop and pray as the Spirit leads you. If you do not yet feel in your heart that you are ready to extend this generosity to her, you need to be honest and confess that to God. He knows your hidden thoughts anyway, so in your own way, ask Him to change *your* heart so that you are ready to make room for Peninnah. Read the prayer, even if you are not yet in agreement.

> *Father, in the Name of Jesus, I lift up my sister _____ and the situation between us. I know that there is nothing hidden from You. You know my heart and every thought that I have had concerning her. I repent of those thoughts and ask that You forgive me for any thoughts, words, or actions that have not been pleasing to You. If I have hurt her in some way that would cause her to act maliciously, I ask that You reveal it to me and humble me so that I may apologize to her so that we may live in the unity and peace to which You have called us as members of Your body. Where _____ is hurting, Father, I ask for her peace and comfort. Minister to her heart in a way that her joy may be restored and she, in turn, will minister joy and peace to others. Mend the broken places in her, Father. And help us, by Your Holy Spirit, to walk in love and peace. In the Name of Jesus I pray. Amen.*

Chapter 3 Ordinary Pain

Your feelings matter. So many well-meaning individuals scold us, insisting that it is not about us, that our feelings are deceptive, that we must undergo trials, and that Jesus warned us of the suffering we must endure. We can easily convince ourselves that we must quietly tolerate every evil thing that is imposed upon us. Any resistance to mistreatment might be viewed by others as complaining, and if they voice their criticism, it can lead to our feeling guilty and belittling ourselves. We also sometimes believe that as Christians we should be above the hurts that others experience.

Those principles of tolerance and suffering are true and are based on Scripture. However, like most principles, their interpretation requires balance. While we are commanded to bear with the failings of the weak (Romans 15:1-6), we also have a responsibility to help the weak become strong (Ephesians 4:11-15). James 1:2-4 states,

> ² Consider it pure joy, my brothers and sisters, whenever you face trials of many kinds,
> ³ because you know that the testing of your faith produces perseverance.
> ⁴ Let perseverance finish its work so that you may be mature and complete, not lacking anything.

This is a reminder that suffering and trials build character and help us become more mature. We will take that further in Chapter 5. For now, we need to be reassured that hurt feelings can cut to the core of who we are and how we see ourselves in relation to others, while we keep in mind that Christians are not to base our lives on feelings, but on truth. Therefore, we need to be reasonable in how we view our pain and mistreatment.

We might differ in our opinions as to what type of behavior can result in woundedness. All of us will not respond in the same manner to the same treatment, so we may have different levels of tolerance and different opinions of just what emotional wounding means. What does it look like? What about extremes? Not only that, but the way we respond to annoyances has a great deal to do with how we already feel about the offender. Think about your closest friend and contrast her with the individual you find very difficult to tolerate. How do bad habits such as chronic lateness or interrupting you when you are speaking strike you differently in one than they do in the other? Do you have the same reaction, regardless of who pushes your buttons?

Several examples or descriptions may be necessary to bring us to a common understanding of just what is meant by the behaviors that wound us. Think about whether or not any of the following behaviors are typical in your relationship with a woman in your fellowship. You may be either the victim or the perpetrator. God knows your heart and its motives.

- cold, brief conversations
- refusing to make eye contact
- pretending not to see or hear her
- not supporting her ministry efforts
- not defending her against open attacks (un-Christlike behavior or words from others)
- not being able to commend her or her good works
- detracting from her character under the pretense of "prayer requests" or "sharing"
- excluding her from ministry or social activities
- failure to make spiritual gifts available to her
- disagreeing with her ideas for no legitimate reason
- gossip and mockery
- sarcasm

- left-handed compliments
- failure to pray for her
- criticism
- . . .

This long list could go on and on. Each time I thought I had listed a broad enough range of examples, I thought of another type of behavior that should be stated specifically. For the victim, some are certainly worse than others, and you can probably add a few that are not listed. There is no one particular description of Peninnah's behavior, other than that her treatment is mean, unloving, and displeasing to Christ. Authors Sue Edwards and Kelley Mathews call her "insensitive, manipulating, or just plain mean."[1] This obviously does not describe more vicious and abusive behaviors that could be dangerous, illegal, or threaten your livelihood or the stability of your family. Those go far beyond the intended scope of this book. If you have been victimized in such a manner, you may need more therapeutic help if you cannot manage and heal from the pain on your own.

The examples in the list might be considered minor annoyances, insignificant and childish

---

1. Taken with permission from *Leading Women Who Wound: Strategies for Effective Ministry* © 2009, by Sue Edwards and Kelley Mathews (Chicago: Moody Publishers), 11.

behavior from someone whom you are mature enough to not give the power to hurt you. However, even minor annoyances can *lead* to emotional wounds, especially since they usually occur as combined and repeated behaviors. For example, few of us would be bothered by someone who refuses to make eye contact with us, even when she is spoken to directly. But the sister who uses this as a means of aggravation and to convey her dislike is also likely to exclude her victim from ministry activities and hurl sarcasm at her, and to do so on a regular basis.

Take another look at Hannah in verses 8 and 10:

> **8** Elkanah her husband would say to her, "Hannah, why are you weeping? Why don't you eat? Why are you downhearted? . . ."
> **10** In bitterness of soul Hannah wept much and prayed to the LORD.

Hannah wept and would not eat. She was hurt and angry. She cried out to God. But she was not what most of us might describe as "over the top" with her pain. She was not suicidal. She did not abandon her service to God. While Peninnah had indeed hit her mark in driving Hannah to tears, Hannah's deepest anguish was due to her childlessness.

The wounds from insensitive and sharp-tongued individuals may cause aggravation, but we should be careful about comparing an insult in the kitchen to the trials that Job suffered. We cannot compare a left-handed compliment such as "I wish I could make my clothes last as long as you do," to the loss of a loved one. The level of annoyance depends on the individual, of course, but should we reasonably call sniping and insults "suffering?"

These behaviors are hurtful. Do not belittle or deny the wound, but do not make it more significant than it is. The tears Hannah cried at Peninnah's agitation were real and deeply felt— Scripture makes that clear. But Peninnah's aggravating behavior was a vicious worsening of Hannah's greater concern, and Hannah seemed to respond as one would reasonably expect.

In *Healing Care Healing Prayer*, seminary professor and author Dr. Terry Wardle discusses what he calls "deep wounds." These are wounds that occurred in our pasts that we have attempted to hide or forget. They "affect people in negative and destructive ways, often sending individuals into deep spiritual, emotional and relational crisis. . . . [They are] ugly, dark and destructive."[2]

---

2. Terry Wardle, *Healing Care Healing Prayer: Helping the Broken Find Wholeness in Christ* (Abilene, TX: Leafwood Publishers, 2001), 13, 45, 189. Used by permission.

Clearly, we should not confuse these deep wounds with the types of wounds that result from the behavior similar to the examples in the list, and we should be able to distinguish between them. Our being responsible to some degree for our own maturity demands that we take a rational view of our hurts and wounds. This is thinking soberly.

Every jab that we endure should not result in a deep wound or even the hurt feelings that linger, change our relationships, and require forgiveness. There are times that we do need to "get over it." Some exchanges should not require forgiveness because they are insignificant. We may simply need to accept that there was a lack of intent or a misunderstanding, or we may just need to grow up. As one sister put it, we need to be bigger than allowing ourselves to be offended because "She hugged me last."

There is a point at which we have to realize that we cannot allow ourselves to be affected by others' petty comments and behavior. This principle may require more attention than I want to give it within these pages, but please try to get this into your head and heart: Do not give *anyone* a more significant role in your life than their value for you deserves.

Chapter 4

Who Is Elkanah?

Bible scholars and theologians differ in their views of Elkanah. He is commended for being a considerate husband by some, while others criticize him for being insensitive and ego driven and suggest that his actions worsened the conflict between Hannah and Peninnah.[1] I tend to agree with the latter group, but with qualifications.

~

Several years ago, long before I recognized that God had placed this burden for emotionally wounded women on my heart, I taught a Bible study on this 1 Samuel passage. When it came

---

1. Ralph W. Klein, *First Samuel*, Word Biblical Commentary 10 (Waco, TX: Word Books, 1982), 7; Mary J. Evans, *1 and 2 Samuel*, New International Biblical Commentary, Old Testament Series (Peabody, MA: Hendrickson Publishers, 2000), 16; David G. Firth, *1 and 2 Samuel*, Apollos Old Testament Commentary (Nottingham, England: Apollos, 2009), 54.

to Elkanah, I remember that those in the class voiced unanimous criticism of his behavior. Women honed in directly on his thoughtlessness toward Hannah. How could this insensitive clod not see that it was *for him* that Hannah wanted children? The men simply realized, perhaps from the reactions of the women, that Elkanah was in trouble.

Elkanah's ineffective leadership was recognized, but it was not the point of the study. The text was not examined in its historical setting. We were looking at the story as a biblical example of the need for contemporary women's ministries, not examining the role or responsibilities of male heads of household in Elkanah and Hannah's polygamous culture.

I did not rake Elkanah over the coals or use his behavior as an opportunity to criticize men. (Christian women should never take up the habit of "male bashing" that is so common in the world, especially in a setting with individuals who are unsaved, and especially when it concerns church leaders.) My explanation for his inconsiderate behavior was an attempt to highlight my point that women understand the hearts of women, just as men minister to and understand men's unique needs in a way that women cannot. I concluded that Elkanah was simply and innocently without a clue as to *how* to comfort Hannah. Therefore, as verse 8 tells us, he led with his ego and was unaware of his error:

> [8] Elkanah her husband would say to her, "Hannah, why are you weeping? Why don't you eat? Why are you downhearted? Don't I mean more to you than ten sons?"

In the midst of her rival's hateful rant, Hannah's husband not only did not understand her, but he scolded her with his sense of his own grandness. On the surface his words may seem to have offered comfort. However, those words most likely would not have translated to "Why are you *downhearted*?" but to "Why are you *resentful*?"[2] Those two words say very different things about Hannah's character. Calling her "downhearted" would have shown that he recognized that she was a victim and had been hurt. But by calling her "resentful," he was actually accusing her of being petty and jealous. Elkanah loved Hannah, and it means a great deal to any woman to be loved by a man. But there was another woman whose presence tortured Hannah—a woman who had been brought into their household to do for her husband what she could not. Women probably have no trouble imagining Hannah's emotional hell.

Another Bible scholar suggests that Elkanah only plays a minor role in this story.[3] He may, but in our modern setting, we need to recognize the role of leadership in healing conflicts. This is

2. Firth, 54.
3. Ibid.

the role that Elkanah might have represented, but in terms of usefulness, it was only on the surface. If we can serve the same purpose that was undertaken in that Bible study—to look at these characters from ancient civilization as models for our present roles—Elkanah should have been the leader and mediator in this conflict between his rival wives. Therefore, his role is not minor at all. It is significant in that as the husband in a male-dominated society, he should have been a more competent leader of his household.

I do not want us to lose sight of our main focus on Hannah and Peninnah's relationship and the healing that needs to take place between their modern day representatives. Still, there is a caution for leaders as this scenario unfolds, and there is a reminder that they may need to become involved in the healing process in disagreements such as these.

Let us turn our attention to Eli, the other leader here. We observe his encounter with Hannah in verses 9 through 17:

> 9 Once when they had finished eating and drinking in Shiloh, Hannah stood up. Now Eli the priest was sitting on a chair by the doorpost of the LORD's temple.
> 10 In bitterness of soul Hannah wept much and prayed to the LORD.
> 11 And she made a vow, saying, "O LORD Almighty, if you will only look upon your servant's misery and remember me, and not forget your servant but give her a

son, then I will give him to the LORD for all the days of his life, and no razor will ever be used on his head."

12 As she kept on praying to the LORD, Eli observed her mouth.

13 Hannah was praying in her heart, and her lips were moving but her voice was not heard. Eli thought she was drunk

14 and said to her, "How long will you keep on getting drunk? Get rid of your wine."

15 "Not so, my lord," Hannah replied, "I am a woman who is deeply troubled. I have not been drinking wine or beer; I was pouring out my soul to the LORD.

16 Do not take your servant for a wicked woman; I have been praying here out of my great anguish and grief."

17 Eli answered, "Go in peace, and may the God of Israel grant you what you have asked of him."

Initially, Eli called the situation inaccurately and in a way that would bring Hannah's character into question. Remember, Hannah's barrenness already cast doubt on her godliness in the eyes of others, and now here was Eli accusing her of being drunk, which Hannah interpreted as wickedness. Look at this woman's misery:

- I am barren.
- That woman is driving me to tears.
- My husband does not understand me.
- My priest thinks I am wicked.

God created us to be male or female. Gender roles and distinctions are real, purposeful, and necessary. Men and women lead differently. Hannah was pouring her heart out; Eli was focused on order. This is not criticism of either of them, but simply recognition that we have different leadership styles. We need to be respectful of those variations in order to lead effectively. Edwards and Mathews recognize our differences and make this point:

> Male ministers tend to handle conflict without taking into account the gender of the parties involved. Big mistake. Men and women process conflict differently. Ignoring the gender factor as you attempt to negotiate differences can severely hamper your effectiveness and lessen the likelihood of a positive outcome.
>
> Do you understand basic differences in the way men and women process conflict? If not, your effectiveness will be [hindered]. You will be expecting women in conflict to act like men, and when they don't, you will be surprised and frustrated.[4]

Eli did come to recognize his error and realize that Hannah was broken and troubled. He blessed her and sent her off in peace. He did well in that regard. Eli has been called spiritually dull and unable to hear from God for his failure to immediately recognize God's call to Samuel (the son Hannah later bore who assisted Eli in the temple).[5] I would not go quite that far, but

---

4. Edwards and Mathews, 152. Taken with permission.
5. Robert D. Bergen, *The New American Commentary* (Nashville, TN: B & H Publishing Group), 58.

there is little disagreement that he was a miserable failure as a parent (1 Samuel 2:12-3:18). I would find it difficult to give him whole-hearted support as an example of leadership. We can view both him and Elkanah as warnings for leaders. The behavior of both of these men shows us some things that leaders should not do and some of the common traps to avoid when ministering to the unique needs of women in conflict.

Practically all of the New Testament letters reveal some type of conflict in the early churches, much of it having to do with personal relationships. Members involved in disagreements of a personal nature stand out in particular in 1 Corinthians. Even where conflicts are not directly identified, the recipients of the letters were urged toward peaceful living (Ephesians 4:2-3; Philippians 4:2; Hebrews 12:14-15). Although conflict is as old as the organized church, it was not until the 1970s that conflict resolution as a ministry began to receive serious attention. Many issues that might have had positive outcomes with a leader's influence have gone unresolved. There is undoubtedly a great deal of pain in the church that is being ignored.

Leaders should be prepared to mediate disagreements, but the types of conflicts under discussion here generally do not come to the attention of church leaders. Part of the reason is the overall silence surrounding women wounding one another, and part is because of the nature of these conflicts.

Ken Sande, president of Peacemaker Ministries, defines *conflict* as "a difference in opinion or purpose that frustrates someone's goals or desires."[6] This may not be the case with many women's disputes. But conflict also means to be at odds or in opposition, which is usually the character of women's clashes. In addition, one of the main *causes* of conflict is the "sinful attitudes and habits that lead to sinful words and actions."[7] Therefore, those habits such as the ones listed in Chapter 3 may appropriately be considered to fall within the category of conflict.

Personal conflicts between women in the church differ in some significant ways from the conflicts that receive more attention. They do not normally grow into congregational issues. Because of the way they are usually handled, the details are often known only to the women who are directly involved (although a larger group will hear bits of gossip or witness the tension and draw their own conclusions). These disputes are not likely to lead to a significant loss of church

---

6. Ken Sande, *The Peacemaker: A Biblical Guide to Resolving Personal Conflict* (Grand Rapids, MI: Baker Books, 2004), 29.

7. Ibid., 30.

income and do not lead to church splits. Such matters are not often brought to the attention of church leaders for the purpose of resolution.

That last point, that such conflicts are not usually brought to the attention of leaders, is helpful if it means that leaders are freed to spend their time in the study of the Word and development of programs that spiritually grow and nurture the congregation and community. It is preferable for the women involved to handle these issues on their own. However, if it means that disagreements are being swept under the rug while members remain at odds with and distant from one another, that is not peace as Christ intended.

This is the same principle expressed in Acts 6, where we first read the circumstances that established the ministry of deacons in the church:

> [1] In those days when the number of disciples was increasing, the Grecian Jews among them complained against the Hebraic Jews because their widows were being overlooked in the daily distribution of food.
> [2] So the Twelve gathered all the disciples together and said, "It would not be right for us to neglect the ministry of the word of God in order to wait on tables.
> [3] Brothers and sisters, choose seven men from among you who are known to be full of the Spirit and wisdom. We will turn this responsibility over to them
> [4] and will give our attention to prayer and the ministry of the word."

Deacons, who are servant leaders, were put in place in response to a conflict that was based on a concrete issue: One group thought another group was receiving better care. The apostles did not want to be distracted from the ministry of spreading the Word of God and advancing the newly established church in order to attend to distributing charitable gifts. This is one of the oldest examples of church conflict. Christ desires harmony between believers, so leaders must be in place to carry out this ministry of resolving issues when needed. Matthew 18:15-17 illustrates this need in the words of Christ Himself:

> 15 If your brother or sister sins against you, go and point out their fault, just between the two of you. If they listen to you, you have won them over.
> 16 But if they will not listen, take one or two others along, so that 'every matter may be established by the testimony of two or three witnesses.'
> 17 If they still refuse to listen, tell it to the church; and if they refuse to listen even to the church, treat them as you would a pagan or a tax collector.

Ideally, women should discuss and resolve their issues of insults or misunderstandings just between the two of them. This is the procedure for settling disputes that Christ laid out. But if they cannot, skilled leaders may be required to intervene. The "one or two others" in verse 16 clearly refers to those qualified to operate in this role. *Qualified* means a number of things in ministry, but above all, it means being called by

God, for which there will be evidence that assures you that they are trustworthy and mature.

We can look backwards through the lens of time and suggest that Elkanah could and should have done *something*. It is obvious that he did nothing to lessen the hostility in the household. It was a difficult situation in which two women were hurt and victimized. Neither a double portion of meat nor turning on the charm was the solution.

Eli also stumbled. His shortcomings as a leader and as a parent were many. Whatever the reason for his response to Hannah's bold denial of his accusation of drunkenness, he demonstrated a heart and a desire to restore a woman who was in pain, and he was willing to retreat from his original position when he realized he had made an error in judging her circumstances. This quality is in high demand for leaders in any setting.

Chapter 5 Accountability

Everyone in the church must be held account-able for her behavior at some level. In most conflicts, we hold the maturing saint responsible for restraint, patience, and love—for demonstrating the fruit of the Spirit according to Galatians 5 and not being vindictive when provoked. We *should* do this. However, when any individual makes mean, petty comments, degrades another's character, belittles someone, or hurts a sister in any way, she should be brought to task for her behavior. Otherwise, we allow that offending woman's growth process to be stunted and delayed.

~

I remember when my nephew Nick was a rambunctious, bouncing, eight- or nine-month-old baby. One day while my mother was holding him, he gleefully raised his chubby little hand and snatched her eyeglasses off of her face, just as any baby will do. Bouncing and playing in her arms, he flung them across the room and shrieked with delight at his game. How do you think she reacted? If you know anything about doting, over-indulgent, first-time grandmothers, you can guess. Taken in by his delight, she thought it was adorable.

But let me pose this question: How would she have reacted if an eight-year-old had done such a thing? She would have been horrified! That child's lack of discipline would have been criticized to anyone who would listen. He would no doubt have been made to apologize. Someone would have insisted that he pick up the glasses, and he would have been lectured and finger-wagged into sorrow. After he returned them to their owner, he probably would have been sent to his room. Allowing for varying styles of discipline, this may not have been the end of his punishment.

Now another question: What if an eight*teen*-year-old had done this? Not only would we all be horrified, but the victim would more than likely feel as if her safety were threatened—fear would probably have been her first reaction. Depending on her relationship to the perpetrator, she may even wonder if legal action should be taken for this assault. She would avoid him and relay his behavior to others who would be equally horrified and duly sympathetic as they advised her as to what course of action she should take. She would never forget and would quite possibly find it difficult to forgive such aggressive and hostile behavior. His presence would bring up an immediate recall of the event, and with each memory feelings of fear, insecurity, and anxiety would arise anew.

Would this be an appropriate response to the eight-year-old perpetrator? Certainly not. And it would be ridiculous to even ask this question with regard to the eight-month-old. All of our responses should be in proportion to the individual's level of maturity, which determines the extent to which we can hold her responsible for her behavior.

So what about the salty-tongued sister who makes an "innocently" insulting remark about your casserole or "casually" observes that your house smells a little fishy? She may be the same sister who never fails to notice when you have put on five pounds, but she ignores or belittles your accomplishments and talents.

Plug this principle into the example of eight-month-old baby Nick throwing my mother's eyeglasses across the room. We cannot even reasonably ask if a baby should be sent to his room. The most one may have expected would be that Grandma may have frowned and shaken her head "No." But can you imagine allowing a child to grow into an eight-year-old who demonstrates this same type of behavior—and thinking it is funny? This is what I mean by one's growth process being malformed. Moreover, probably anyone who heard of this eight-year-old's behavior would question his parents' responsibility, not his. Someone failed to provide the upbringing and guidance the child needed in order to develop properly.

The same thing is true of spiritual maturity. We can never force an individual's spiritual growth to conform to our personal standards. However, Christ's intention for believers to grow spiritually is clear. The Apostle Paul wrote to a church that was fairly new, yet the expectation was that the converts should have become, in whatever amount of time had passed, more mature than they were.

1 Corinthians 3:1-3

> [1] Brothers and sisters, I could not address you as people who live by the Spirit but as people who are still worldly—mere infants in Christ.
> [2] I gave you milk, not solid food, for you were not yet ready for it. Indeed, you are still not ready.
> [3] You are still worldly. For since there is jealousy and quarreling among you, are you not worldly? Are you not acting like mere humans?

The members of the Corinthian church were still trapped in worldly thinking and behavior. Instead of relationships that reflected humility and respectful treatment of one another, there was bickering and self-centeredness. This is unbecoming of Christians and is the breeding ground for personal conflict.

The Holy Spirit inspired the author of Hebrews to address the same matter:

Hebrews 5:11-14

> 11 We have much to say about this, but it is hard to make it clear to you because you no longer try to understand.
> 12 In fact, though by this time you ought to be teachers, you need someone to teach you the elementary truths of God's word all over again. You need milk, not solid food!
> 13 Anyone who lives on milk, being still an infant, is not acquainted with the teaching about righteousness.
> 14 But solid food is for the mature, who by constant use have trained themselves to distinguish good from evil.

The recipients of this letter apparently had been Christians for a considerable amount of time, since the author uses the phrase "by this time" in verse 12. Yet, they seem to have had no interest in moving on in their spiritual growth and were content to remain infants. The warnings tell us that this is just not acceptable.

There is nothing wrong with being an immature Christian. In fact, it is a wonderful position to be in, but only for a time. It means that so many things are new: the acceptance of faith, the questions, the church relationships, the attempt at understanding the Word of God, and the zeal with which we share our new life with others. All of these experiences energize us and encourage us onward in what should be a joyous walk with our Savior.

However, there is something wrong with remaining immature. This does not mean that we should attempt to measure another individual's spiritual growth against a checklist and a calendar, but Christ expects increasing maturity in our walk with Him.

Let me add this to the caution against remaining immature in our faith: There is also something wrong with our allowing our sisters to remain spiritual infants. We will stunt the spiritual growth of the immature saint if we do not hold her accountable for her behavior, and constantly expect the maturing saint to "be the bigger person" or "take the high road." Expecting more from a mature individual is reasonable, but we should not continuously heap abuse upon her as if her progressive walk with Christ should bring her misery at the hands of other Christians. How will the immature saint ever grow? Just as we would hold the parents of that eight-year-old responsible for his behavior, more mature believers must hold new or immature believers accountable for becoming Christlike.

Wounds are often inflicted by women who are spiritually immature. They are not behaving in a Christlike manner when they intentionally wound others, no matter how long they have

been saved or their positions in the church. The-
ologian Dr. Tony Evans states,

> [Maturity] is coming to the place where you
> think, judge, and react biblically to every sit-
> uation. When it is the rule and not the excep-
> tion for you to apply the Bible to your life;
> when you place every area of your life under
> the lordship of Jesus Christ; when you can
> say in everything, "Here I am, Lord. What do
> You want me to do?"—then you are a mature
> disciple of Jesus Christ. The Bible calls it
> Christlikeness, because Jesus is intent on
> making you like Him.[1]

We cannot pronounce a woman "immature"
simply because she makes an inappropriate
comment. So-called mature Christians also have
lapses into spiritual infancy. They tire of being
the bigger person and they also struggle with
their flesh. But those lapses should be brief and
infrequent; the conviction of the indwelling Holy
Spirit will not let them be comfortable in that
place for long. They probably will not require too
much assistance or support from others to find
their way back on track. On the other hand, if it
is normal for a sister to make offensive com-

---

1. Taken from *Time to Get Serious: Daily Devotions to
Keep You Close to God*, by Tony Evans, © 1995, p. 205.
Used by permission of Crossway, a publishing ministry of
Good News Publishers, Wheaton, IL. www.crossway.org.

ments and communicate negatively with others, this is certainly not the Christ-likeness that marks spiritual maturity, and might call her maturity into question. James 1:26 supports this view:

> 26 Those who consider themselves religious and yet do not keep a tight rein on their tongues deceive themselves, and their religion is worthless.[2]

The word *religious* is used to refer to outward appearances that might be mistaken for maturity, such as regular church attendance and refraining from certain behaviors. But the point is that such virtuous behavior is meaningless if that sister will not control her tongue, not only from mean-spirited comments, but from other sins in which the tongue is the culprit, such as gossip and slander—the frequent tools of emotional wounding.

Regardless of where we are in our faith in terms of the number of years we have been saved, our roles in church, or how much we think we know, our spiritual journey should never end. When we cooperate with the Holy Spirit, He leads us through the lifelong process

---

2. James 3:1-12 elaborates on the need to control one's tongue.

of sanctification. In Philippians 2:12-13 Paul states,

> 12 Therefore, my dear friends, as you have always obeyed—not only in my presence, but now much more in my absence—continue to work out your salvation with fear and trembling,
> 13 for it is God who works in you to will and to act in order to fulfill his good purpose.

We should never think that our spiritual growth is complete. God's work in us is continuous when we choose to submit to His will.

~

"I was just wondering: Are you swollen, or are you overweight?"

I was overweight—at least 100 pounds overweight. Probably fifty pounds lighter than my heaviest adult weight, but still, miserably, 100 pounds overweight. The woman who asked me this question was not an innocent child; she was at least sixty years old, a Sunday school teacher from another church.

Women who would call themselves spiritually mature or matur*ing* can also be guilty of wounding others. In our zeal to become mature saints, we too often seek after facts *about* God. We become skilled at quoting Scripture and memorizing biblical history. We wrap ourselves in what we think are the correct behaviors, conversations, and service to the church. This type of conformity may be an *outworking* of your faith. Because of our love for Christ and a desire to please Him, our interests should and do change. But we also neglect some of the most simple and basic commands in Scripture, such as "Do unto others" and "Love your neighbor" (Matthew 7:12; 22:39). We must strive not only to please Christ with our outward behavior, but to imitate His character. In other words, we are not just *doing*, but *being*.

When the Sunday school teacher hurled her vicious insult at me, I was shocked, hurt, and caught off-guard, so I said nothing. Please do not practice vindictive, snappy, comeback lines for the next time your Peninnah vexes your spirit. That is *not* the intent of "Do unto others." In fact, it was probably best that I did not respond in any way at the time. I was hurt and angered by the woman's comment, but I could not react then, because she had stopped me as I was on my way to lead worship. Still, I should have voiced my concern later, and I cannot help but believe that many more women would have been spared her insults if I had *lovingly* cautioned her about her hurtful words.

Not holding one another accountable is cowardly and self-indulgent—the easy way out. So how should this woman have been approached? In Ephesians 4 Paul teaches us some principles of maturity and unity:

14 Then we will no longer be infants, tossed back and forth by the waves, and blown here and there by every wind of teaching and by the cunning and craftiness of people in their deceitful scheming.
15 Instead, speaking the truth in love, we will in all things grow up into him who is the head, that is, Christ.
16 From him the whole body, joined and held together by every supporting ligament, grows and builds itself up in love, as each part does its work.

The situations that I have personally experienced or those that have been shared with me by other women regarding wounding and being wounded frequently involve women whom one would presume to be mature: Sunday school teachers, choir directors, and ministry leaders. Spiritual maturity is not attained by knowledge of Scripture, length of service, or leadership position *alone*. All of these factors, combined with others, may be important to the development of a mature saint, but they do not define maturity. Spiritual maturity is determined by our Christ-likeness.[3]

Christ would have His people to be unified and spiritually mature. Because He is truth, our relationships with one another should be based on truth and honesty. When we speak the truth in love, we do just that: Motivated by love and a desire to see one another grow, we honestly ad-

---

3. Terry Wardle, *Outrageous Love Transforming Power: How the Holy Spirit Shapes You into the Likeness of Christ* (Abilene, TX: Leafwood Publishers, 2004), 11.

dress difficult situations. All of us who claim to have a relationship with Him should have a desire to see wounding behavior among women in the church stop. Ignoring the habit in other women is not in anyone's best interest, and we should certainly not want to be guilty of it ourselves.

Members of the church are expected to confront one another regarding sin, which includes intentional offenses. The stated goal in Matthew 18:15-17 is for restoration of relationships, not seeking revenge, making accusations, or punishing a guilty party. Only when we confront the offender in love can restoration be accomplished. Winning the offender over helps her see her error. Being able to admit wrong-doing is a crucial step in the growth process. Unfortunately, the correction we wish to exercise sometimes has a self-serving and proud motive. Our purpose is not *restoration* but *condemnation* if we take an offender to task but have no interest in helping her recognize the error of her ways and repent.

We need to be honest with ourselves and with God about our intentions and responsibility in our relationships with our sisters. He knows our hearts. Look at the scenario in Mark 2:8 when Jesus encountered the Pharisees who were trying to find a reason to condemn Him:

8 Immediately Jesus knew in his spirit that this was what they were thinking in their hearts, and he said to them, "Why are you thinking these things?"

David said to God in Psalm 139,

2 You know when I sit and when I rise; you perceive my thoughts from afar.
3 You discern my going out and my lying down; you are familiar with all my ways.
4 Before a word is on my tongue you know it completely, O Lord.

There are two very important audiences here. My motivation for writing this book is not only to acknowledge the pain of the Hannahs in the church. I also believe that there are many of Hannah's sisters who will read it and recognize the Peninnah spirit that has gripped them, and they will be broken by their sin and allow God to change their hearts. They may recall an instance from long ago or they may be honest enough to confess that it is their regular pattern for relating to a certain woman in their fellowship, and they will allow the power of the Holy Spirit to convict and change them. In verses 23-24 David continued,

23 Search me, O God, and know my heart; test me and know my anxious thoughts.
24 See if there is any offensive way in me, and lead me in the way everlasting.

We will not grow unless we stop lying to ourselves and to God. We must confess, examine our hearts and our ways, repent to God, and probably offer one or two apologies to our sisters.

It is difficult to admit that we wound others. As Christian women, we are not supposed to be petty or mean. Fortunately, we usually do not engage in the level of cut-throat, vicious, and potentially dangerous wounding (for example, sabotaging careers) that occurs in the world. But we sometimes bring some of the same worldly attitudes from the world to the church. Too often, we try to conceal, deny, or defend those attitudes rather than allow our thinking to be transformed and renewed (Romans 12:1-3).

We are only deceiving ourselves when we do not admit that we, too, have wounded with our mouths and with our behavior. I want to stop now and pray for those of you who recognize yourselves.

> *Father, in the Name of Your Son Jesus, I lift up to You my wonderful sister who is confessing that she has related to her sisters in a way that we know is not pleasing to You. I thank You for her humbling herself before You, Father. Thank You for her courage, and thank You for Your never-ending love and forgiveness. I ask that You would help her show love and kindness to those she has hurt with her words or behavior,*

and that You would continually bring her before You to seek Your strength and Your Holy Spirit empowerment for continued victory in this area, that she may be pleasing in Your sight. In the Name of Jesus, I pray for her and in agreement with her. Amen.

~

If Elkanah had questioned Peninnah about her treatment of Hannah, we can take a guess as to any number of likely responses from her. In our culture, they may range from defensiveness (*You're always accusing me of something! Nothing I do pleases you!*) to blame (*Why do you always take her side? You gave her twice as much as you gave me! She thinks she's better than me!*) to denial (*Who, me? No, honey, I'm sorry, but she must have misunderstood*). Despite their protests when confronted with their behavior, their eyes, tone, body language, and the behavior that resumes almost immediately after that confrontation all tell a different story. Many will claim that we cannot trust these signals: "You can't read my mind," they might insist. No, sister, I can't, but I know how you treat me!

When questioned about their offensive behavior and asked for an admission or explanation, many women will deny that a problem exists, even if the relationship is marked by tension:

Oh no, nothing's wrong . . .
No, you haven't done anything . . .

This highlights an interesting point that one Bible commentator makes regarding Hannah and Peninnah. The Hebrew terms that are used to describe Peninnah's irritation of Hannah imply that it is not Peninnah's intent to elicit anger from Hannah, but to cause "inward commotion."[4]

Peninnahs usually do not want an open conflict. The damage they do is to cause inner turmoil that leaves no visible wounds or damage that you can easily identify. To compound this problem, women generally tend to avoid direct confrontation; we express our offense as *indirect* anger,[5] such as being sullen, irritable, or as we say, having an "attitude." So we have turmoil festering in two individuals who may be inwardly seething, yet they ignore the tension. When an issue has not been acknowledged, it cannot be resolved. We need to be courageous and humble enough to admit when there is a problem in communicating with our sisters.

Have you ever tried to be in a relationship with someone who was *fundamentally* different

---

4. C.F. Keil and F. Delitzsch, *Joshua, Judges, Ruth, 1 and 2 Samuel.* Vol. 2 of *Commentary on the Old Testament* (Peabody, MA: Hendrickson Publishers, Inc., 2006), 243.

5. Edwards and Mathews, 32-33.

from you? This is not a matter of trying to be compatible with someone who likes action movies, but you prefer comedies. What you are fundamentally is what makes you "you." It is the basis and core of who you are. The Word tells us repeatedly that God is truth (Deuteronomy 32:4; Psalm 33:4; John 14:6; 18:37). Since you are in a relationship with Him, a persistent, unspoken lie in your relationship with others is in direct conflict with Him. Does it matter if your lie is to yourself? Does it matter if your lie is the easy way to try to maintain that flimsy pretense of "peace" between yourself and others? Yes, it does.

So, recovering Peninnahs, what will you say when Hannah asks, "Have I done something to offend you?"

~

A church leader (whom I will call Diane) went through a period of being emotionally distant from a woman in her congregation (whom I will call Cheryl) with whom she had once enjoyed a close, loving relationship. Diane had been deeply hurt, and, she believed, disrespected by Cheryl for several years. Cheryl knew by Diane's increasing silence and withdrawal from her that something had changed.

Diane was in a dilemma as to how to proceed in their relationship. Because of her role in the church, she wrongly believed that protecting the integrity of church leadership and quietly sacrificing her pride for what she thought was unity meant being non-confrontational (at least in that matter). She thought she should simply remain silent and accept the mistreatment for the sake of her role. If she had acted in true humility, though, Cheryl never would have had any idea that Diane had taken offense to her treatment, although that would not have been the correct response from a leader, either.

The dishonesty in their relationship troubled Diane. If it had been a casual or temporary meeting, her response to Cheryl probably would have been different. She certainly was mature enough to not have been significantly impacted by a brief encounter. But this was a relationship that mattered to her. She was a leader in the church; as such, she needed to be transparent and approachable to everyone.

Pretending to ignore an issue, yet barely tolerating another individual's presence does not translate into peace, and it certainly is not love. God was not pleased. Diane was soothing her offense by being sullen and hostile and avoiding any interaction with Cheryl. This is not suffering in silence; her attitude was revealed by her behavior, which was loud and clear.

After Diane's absence for several weeks, Cheryl finally approached her with the question, "Diane, are we all right?" Cheryl is to be commended for her courage and honesty. When we have been wounded, it is our responsibility to go to the individual who has hurt us to resolve the issue. Diane, having been offended, should have been the one to bring it up. However, Cheryl was aware that her behavior had caused friction, so there was equal responsibility.

Cheryl approached Diane because in response to having been offended, Diane actually became defensive and vindictive by trying, as much as possible, to avoid Cheryl's contempt. She wounded Cheryl in response to being wounded by her, becoming, like Peninnah, a guilty victim. Diane claimed that she wanted to keep peace. She may have, but she also wanted to express her anger without confronting the source. She demonstrated quite clearly a behavior that psychologist and Bible teacher Dr. Larry Crabb describes in *The Safest Place on Earth*:

> When we're abused or rejected or criticized, we don't look at these painful experiences as reason to more clearly depend on God and demonstrate His character in the midst of them. Instead, they become the basis for our figuring out how to live. We *interpret* life experiences, we process them to see how various things make us feel so we can make important decisions about how to live.[6]

---

6. Larry Crabb, *The Safest Place on Earth: Where People Connect and Are Forever Changed* (Nashville, TN: W

This takes us back to the feelings-versus-truth point raised in Chapter 3. Diane, as many of us do, allowed her feelings to determine how she would live in relationship with Cheryl, instead of depending on the truth of God's Word and living and behaving according to His expectations.

If you have been dodging Peninnah's darts for a while, either by avoiding her completely or by trying to ignore her behavior, you have the wrong idea about what peace really means. Peace is not necessarily the *absence* of conflict; peace is the *purpose* of addressing conflict. That means holding one another accountable. If a matter is not resolved in your heart, you need to summon the courage to bring it up to your sister in order to lovingly restore your relationship and help her grow. To do so may require guidance from someone else (without revealing details, harming the other person's character, or the risk of spreading gossip), but you need to do what is necessary according to Scripture in order to achieve real peace.

When confronted, Diane was finally honest with Cheryl about her feelings. Both women took the opportunity to confess, repent, and apolo-

Publishing Group, 1999), 91. Reprinted by permission. Thomas Nelson Inc., Nashville, TN. All rights reserved.

gize, thereby helping one another grow (Hebrews 10:24).

I relayed an incident in Chapter 2 about a church leader who humiliated me in a class. For several minutes at the end of the game, the instructor was wrapping up and asked for our thoughts on the process. I was angry and still shocked, so I did not say anything about what the woman had said to me. Hurt? Yes, and rightfully so. Still, my silence was cowardly. I clearly remember thinking at the time that I did not want any additional attention brought to myself. It was easier to sit in misery knowing that my humiliation would pass, than it would have been to re-focus the attention of the entire class on my pain.

But that painful comment was a perfect teaching opportunity, given the purpose of the class. We were there to discuss leadership and how we respond to issues and conflicts in our congregations. What better time for me to point out how hurtful our words can be and how important it is for us to tackle difficult matters head-on? Instead, for several weeks afterward, I played the tape in my head and nursed my anger.

It would have been so much more fruitful to have taken up the matter either in that teaching moment or later, when I could have taken the offender aside and gently helped her see how inappropriate her words were. Good could have come from that unfortunate incident. She could have grown, and I could have helped her, just as at times I have needed help with spiritual growth. This sister needed to be held accountable for her words, and I missed an opportunity to fulfill my Ephesians 4 responsibility.

I have had my challenges with remaining silent when I should have spoken out. I know how difficult it can be. We even use Scripture to defend our refusal to take this difficult step.

I had a conversation with a sister in which she tearfully expressed the pain she felt as a result of snide remarks from her pastor's wife. "I can't," she wailed, when I tried to convince her that she could only heal her relationship with the woman by confronting her. Later, she came back with more complaints and a Scripture that she felt made her the bigger person in their relationship. Her misunderstanding of Jesus' words in Matthew 5:39 convinced her to submit to what she described as harsh and unkind words from a woman who should have known better.

> **39** But I tell you, do not resist an evil person. If anyone strikes you on the right cheek, turn to them the other cheek also.

Her misinterpretation highlights my point about balancing the need for tolerance with the need to hold others accountable and help them grow. Allow Scripture to interpret Scripture. This passage (including vv. 38-42) refers to Old Testament laws that forbid vindictiveness. It teaches that we should not retaliate beyond the offense and that we are to remain humble and not necessarily claim our "rights." But it does not teach that mistreatment should not be corrected.

There are also times that we should *not* address the hurts imposed by others. For example,

- Is she in the midst of extreme circumstances, such as grief or job loss?
- Is it an isolated incident, out of character for the sister as you know her?
- Are you able to let the incident pass without it (negatively) changing your relationship? Without bringing it up to others? Without vindictiveness? Without acting like a martyr?

There needs to be some combination of these factors in order to justify letting the incident go. It would be grossly insensitive to question someone about a thoughtless remark who has just lost a loved one. But if it is an individual who has a history of wounding you or others with mean comments, it is likely that her behavior has already gone too far, and at some point in the future she will need someone who can speak the truth to her—in love, of course!

Just as we have been Hannahs, most of us have also been Peninnahs. Admit it. One of the most difficult aspects of writing this book was acknowledging my own guilt in this dilemma. To my shame and horror, I recall that on a few occasions in a church I formerly attended, I criticized and mocked a sister behind her back. She had done nothing to warrant my scorn, but for no reason, I joined other women in making unkind remarks about her personal choices.

In that circle of agitators of which I was a part, there were a few who were quite knowledgeable in the Word, had been saved for many years, and were very active in their service to the church—in other words, others might have called them mature. I was a spiritual infant at the time. In no way will I take any opportunity now to make excuses for my past behavior. However, I discovered in my association with them that *all of those women* had been wounded in relationships with women in that church or others. That particular church was a hotbed of gossip and pettiness led by women who had been saved for many years and had been placed in leadership roles. There was bickering and meanness there that far exceeded any that I had experienced in my secular workplace.

Looking back, I wish that any one of those women who knew the Word and very clearly were seeking a closer walk with Christ had taken advantage of the teaching opportunity that my infancy provided. She need have done nothing more than point out that whether our victim was there to hear our vicious words or not, our conduct was out of line. We were doing damage to her, ourselves, and the church. I have no doubt that I would have been ashamed of myself. I hope that I would have changed my behavior.

Maturity demands accountability.

Chapter 6   The Love Covering

If we are going to insist that Peninnahs be held accountable for their behavior because it is essential to their spiritual maturity, we must also be willing to be held accountable for our own growth.

One of the most basic principles for Christian growth is found in John 13:34-35.

> 34 A new command I give you: Love one another. As I have loved you, so you must love one another.
> 35 By this everyone will know that you are my disciples, if you love one another.

The Greek words translated as *love* in the New Testament are *philēo* (or *philadelphia*, a form of the same word), which expresses brotherly love; and *agapē* (or *agapaō*), which expresses sacrificial love. The love that Christ has for His people is often translated from the word meaning brotherly love: "Those whom I [*philēo*] I rebuke and discipline" (Revelation 3:19). In a few instances, the writers of the epistles call upon believers to *philadelphia* one another (Romans 12:10; Hebrews 13:1; 1 Peter 1:22; 2 Peter 1:7). In the Gospels, however, Jesus uses only the word meaning sacrificial love when He tells us how we should treat one another, as in the passage from John which would read,

> **34** A new command I give you: [Agapaō] one another. As I have [agapaō] you, so you must [agapaō] one another. **35** By this everyone will know that you are my disciples, if you [agapē] one another.

The scenario in which Jesus issued the command for us to *agapaō* one another in John 13:34 began with Him washing the feet of His disciples (vv. 1-14). He went on to very strongly urge them to do the same for one another. Our willingness to humbly perform the most menial service for one another is an expression of our sacrificial love. Ego gets in the way of our humbling ourselves to *be like Christ*—doing what He did—loving as He loved.

Christians very often assume that their identity is formed by activities such as church attendance or refraining from certain behaviors: "I don't smoke, drink, go to bars, or curse, so as you can see, I am a Christian." But Christ set a single mark for our Christian identity in the world, which is our love for one another; and our love for one another is based on our love for

Him. If we love Him, seeing His image reflected in the difficult women we fellowship with should shape our relationship with them. When we love God we want to please Him, just as our desire to please a mate or parent is normally rooted in love.

Christ was well acquainted with the types of conflicts that might arise between believers; He had mediated some of them Himself (Matthew 26:6-13; Luke 10:38-42). Nevertheless, the love command from the Old Testament (Leviticus 19:18) was restated with new empowerment— that empowerment being His love for us. The behavior of unworthy recipients did not get in the way of His sacrificial love, so we cannot claim that our sisters' ugly behavior is an excuse for us to not love them. Remember, Christian maturity is marked by our Christ-likeness, not by our performing services.

We would also do well to remember that Satan delights in conflict. As the author of confusion (1 Corinthians 14:33), he takes pleasure in seeing Christ's body (the church) thrown into turmoil, whether it is in the bickering of two sisters or an entire congregation beset by disorder. Scripture tells us that our fight is not against another sister, but against the devil using her to accomplish his purpose. Ephesians 6:12 and 2 Corinthians 10:4 remind us that this is a spiritual battle. You cannot fight a spiritual battle

with fleshly (worldly) weapons, such as vindictiveness and anger.

> 12 For our struggle is not against flesh and blood, but
> against the rulers, against the authorities, against the
> powers of this dark world and against the spiritual
> forces of evil in the heavenly realms.

> 4 The weapons we fight with are not the weapons of the
> world. On the contrary, they have divine power to de-
> molish strongholds.

A stronghold is anything that stubbornly resists
God's will and authority. Whether the stronghold
is your sister's mouth or the way you respond
when you are provoked, love is a powerful spiritual weapon.

Despite any issues that make loving one another difficult—toxic personalities, unworthi-
ness, ugly behavior, or the devil's busyness—we
have a command. *Agapē* does not give us the option of loving only those whom we feel are worthy, or only those who love us the way we want
to be loved. That type of love is *erōs*, which is
passionate or sensual love and is mutual between the giver and recipient. That word is never
used in Scripture. Christ's expectation is that we
make a decision to obey His command to *agapē*
just as we should obey any other command. Our
obedience is reflected in our *doing* what is commanded, not in how we *feel*.

In Chapter 2 just before I prayed in agreement with you for Hannah's sisters, I asked the

Hannahs to confess if they were not ready to forgive their Peninnahs. I hope you understand how important that step is in forgiveness.

There are volumes written on the subject of forgiveness, and the concept is frequently taught in sermons and Bible study classes. It is not my intention to re-teach it here, but I do wish to comment on a principle of God's will in general and forgiveness in particular, which is not usually considered when the subject is raised. That is, we need to honest about our opinions and responses that are outside of God's will, and be willing to pray ourselves *into* His will. In other words, you do not have the right to not forgive your sister or to not love her, and you need to recognize that you are in disobedience if you choose to remain unforgiving and unloving.

Side with God about your error, and especially where you might influence other people and cause them to stumble, keep your mouth closed about your ungodly opinion. If you cannot do that, you should be willing to confess to your hearers that you know that your position is not in keeping with God's will but that you have surrendered to Him for change (hopefully, that is the case). This is true of any matter in which our opinions do not line up with God's Word.

Let me give you an example: God's Word is clear about abortion; debating that is not my purpose here. From the Old Testament to the New Testament, God uses the same word to refer to a fetus as He does a child.[1] He is life, and as such, taking the life of a child is contrary to His nature. Still, there are Christians who adamantly defend their "pro-choice" position, even though it is in disagreement with His. Whenever we have an opinion that opposes what God has said about a matter, we need to pray for Him to bring that opinion in line with His will. If we are serious about growing, we will be willing to do just that—about *all* matters. Meanwhile, be careful about sharing such an opinion with others, or if you do, confess that it is not the biblical view.

I believe that very often we know when we are outside of God's will, but our stubborn pride or burning flesh grips us in disobedience. This is where we need to confess to God that indeed, His ways are not our ways, we know that our own way is wicked, but we remain weak, gripped in sin, and need Him to change our desires. He wants us to be honest about our need for the transforming power of the Holy Spirit to work in us, rather than be arrogant, proud, and defiant, stubbornly holding on to our own will above His.

The issue here is not about the choice we make to remain unloving to a sister, but whether

---

1. The word is *yeled* in the Old Testament. Compare Exodus 1:17 with Exodus 21:22 (KJV). In the New Testament, the word is *brephos*. Compare Luke 1:41 with Luke 18:15.

or not we will submit to His holiness and perfection and place His will above our own. I cannot overstate the fact that God knows our hearts and deeply desires that we be honest with Him. He knows when we are enjoying our sins and are not ready to repent. He knows when we are not walking in love toward a sister just because we are "not feeling it." We need to pray and surrender and allow Him to bring our desires in line with His will.

Relationships normally vary in affection and warmth, even where there is no conflict. But where tension is brewing, you often have a woman who is not a bad-tempered shrew who devours everyone in her path with an equal outpouring of venom. She may be all smiles, sweetness, and encouragement for someone else, but she has chosen you as her victim.

We sometimes have what we like to call "personality conflicts." That phrase is no more than a nice way of saying "I don't have a reason; I just don't like her." But "I don't like her" sounds childish and un-Christlike. We seem to think that if we say we have personality conflicts, it somehow makes our disliking a sister more acceptable.

God has made us unique in our thinking and personal preferences. *Unity* does not mean *uniformity*—we should be one, but we do not have to be the same. Our personalities will conflict with others, and that is not necessarily a bad thing. The problem is that we have not learned how to dislike a sister, yet love her because we say that we love God, and He loves her. We dislike her, so we respond to her like something disgusting we stepped in by accident. We have not learned how to set aside our emotions and pride for God's honor and treat her with genuine kindness.

Go back to that list of behaviors in Chapter 3 (pp. 35-36) that we said frequently describe Peninnah. Do you recognize the presence of one (or more) of them in certain relationships? This is how we tend to treat those we dislike. If we were able to "love her but not like her," none of those behaviors would be evident. If you really loved her, she would never know that you dislike her. Remember Cheryl and Diane? Cheryl knew that Diane had negative feelings toward her because Diane was not behaving in a loving way. If she had been, Cheryl never would have suspected that there was a problem. Again, our aim should not be to hide our feelings, but to submit them to God to change them. My point is that when we don't like someone, very rarely do we treat them as if we love them.

We should be honest and unpretentious in our relationships. There is a very important element in that "Shut up Peninnah" reprimand in Chapter 2. Our goal is not to sweep our true feelings under a spiritual rug so that we all merely tolerate one another and get along—on the outside. Our goal is to make a decision to *agapē* one another so that what comes forth from the heart does, indeed, build us all up.

Paul's words to the church in Colossians 3:12-15 are recalled here, particularly from verse 13:

> **12** Therefore, as God's chosen people, holy and dearly loved, clothe yourselves with compassion, kindness, humility, gentleness and patience.
> **13** Bear with each other and forgive whatever grievances you may have against one another. Forgive as the Lord forgave you.
> **14** And over all these virtues put on love, which binds them all together in perfect unity.
> **15** Let the peace of Christ rule in your hearts, since as members of one body you were called to peace. And be thankful.

This passage speaks of God's desire for us to function in unity and peace. All of these qualities increase when they are motivated by love.

Jesus simply does not change His position that we are to maintain loving fellowship with one another by *doing* sacrificial love. He expects us to love our sisters sacrificially because that is how He loves us, and we are also to love them *as we love ourselves* (Matthew 22:36-39):

> **36** "Teacher, which is the greatest commandment in the Law?"
> **37** Jesus replied: "'Love the Lord your God with all your heart and with all your soul and with all your mind.'
> **38** This is the first and greatest commandment.

[39] And the second is like it: 'Love your neighbor as yourself.' "

This command says something quite powerful. One way of looking at it is to suppose that the same things that we want for ourselves, including prosperity, health, happy families, contentment, peace, and so on, should be the things we want for our sisters. This is true, but it is a little too narrow. Our wanting those things is not necessarily an indicator that we love ourselves; we are naturally inclined to desire those things that provide physical, material, and emotional comfort. Sadly, we all know people who do not know how to love themselves in a healthy way, but they tend to want those things, too. It is also possible to distort that notion of loving yourself and take it to the extremes of selfishness, arrogance, and over-indulging your whims.

Jesus expects us to love ourselves. We are created in His image, and He loves us.[2] His sacrificial death shows us just how much. Since He loved us enough to endure the agony of the cross for us, how can we not love ourselves? That truth should help us grow up in Christ so that even if we dislike a sister, we are able to find something in her to love and value because

2. Briefly, being created in the image of God means that we were created to reflect His characteristics. We bear His image despite the effects of sin when we are redeemed by Christ (Ephesians 4:24; James 3:9).

of the image of God that she reflects. Extend Christian love and sisterly unity even if you think she is too loud, a know-it-all, her voice is irritating, she is boastful, she wears her skirts too short, she thinks she's _____ (fill in the blank), or you don't know, you just don't like her. It is all right if you do not like her, but love her as you love yourself, and treat her as you would want to be treated. That is how we *really* love a sister.

~

When students begin the doctoral program at the seminary I attended, they are assigned an advisor. The advisor's role, as I understood it, was to support the student through the doctoral process. They may advise students about courses, scheduling, and resources. Their job is not to hold the students' hands and lead them. At the point at which they begin writing their proposals and then their dissertations, though, the advisor's role becomes more critical.

I depended on my advisor very little through my course work. We had what I thought was a pleasant relationship. I contacted her only once or twice about the availability of courses or their relevance to my program, and even when she referred my questions to someone else, I felt that I was well advised. She was helpful, and I told her that.

By the time I began writing my proposal, the program had been through several changes of leadership. What advisors were told by one director may have been different from another director's expectations. I was under the impression that the instructor of the proposal class was the only one who would approve my proposal. I later discovered that others in the class had that same understanding.

Four days before my proposal was due, I contacted my advisor by e-mail. I knew that I was going to have to work until the very last minute in order to finish by the deadline. I could not expect her to read it in its entirety and make comments prior to my submitting it. At that time, I had only two or three sections completed, and other sections were done in part. I asked her if she would look at the few sections that were completed, and since rewriting the proposal is a given, I hoped that she would give me pointers for the rewrite.

She fired back that no student ever submits a proposal without the advisor signing off on it and that we needed to talk. When I replied that I may be mistaken but that I had been given very different information, she stated that yes, I was mistaken, repeated that we needed to talk, and that I should call her the following day. I agreed that we needed to talk, and I asked her to send me her telephone number (we had both moved since the last time we had spoken by phone; as I said, we had had very little contact). She then told me that I needed an advisor, to contact the program director, and that she would not discuss it further. I was stunned.

When I contacted the program director the following morning, he apologized profusely for not having told me that two months earlier, my advisor had told him that we had "personality conflicts" and that she had decided that she would no longer advise me.

Four days before what, at that time, was the most critical moment in my academic career, and the person who was supposed to have been on that road with me coldly and abruptly severed our relationship because she disliked me for *no reason* (the true meaning of "personality conflicts"), and then pretended that she still had some authority in that process. For a brief period, I was gripped by anger and confusion. This woman—a Christian, a church leader, my sister in Christ, supposedly a woman who was "spiritually mature"—yet she could not get past such a petty, ungodly, juvenile self-indulgence and guide me through the process, as was her duty.

But I grew from that experience and was forever changed by it. What the devil means for evil, we must allow God to use for good (Genesis 50:19-20). My anger soon passed, and I resolved at that time that I would never treat anyone the way my former advisor had treated me. I pray that if I am ever tempted to the brink of being dismissive and superior toward others or intentionally hurting them with my attitude toward them, that I will remember how un-Christlike and deceptive this woman was in her treatment of me. Whether I choose to spend an afternoon with a sister or not, I will love her and encourage her because I love Jesus, and He commands me to do so without making a judgment as to whether or not our personalities are compatible.

Don't lose sight of that point. Most of us have been hurt by what feels like the intentional daggers of others. Few of us put those feelings away without a great deal of spiritual wrestling. Our own experiences should give us the sensitivity to never want to hurt anyone the way we have been hurt. Let Paul's words from Colossians 3:12-13 overtake you and shape you into spiritual maturity—the likeness of Christ.

> 12 Therefore, as God's chosen people, holy and dearly loved, clothe yourselves with compassion, kindness, humility, gentleness and patience.
> 13 Bear with each other and forgive whatever grievances you may have against one another. Forgive as the Lord forgave you.

When we are in a relationship with Jesus Christ (chosen, holy, and loved)—in other words, when we claim that He is our Lord and Savior, the Head of our lives—we are required to put on the virtues that Paul lists in verse 12. Those qualities are tested in us when we are insulted and vexed. This is true when the perpetrator may not have intended or been aware of the offense, and it is just as true in an extreme case of being viciously and intentionally wounded, as Hannah was by Peninnah. Here is our call to "bear with" those whose faults or unpleasant traits become irritants to us (v. 13). This is what we do with personality conflicts.

So many minor issues become major thorns in relationships. This is because we do not know how to disagree, especially strongly or publicly, and move on without our relationships being affected, and we certainly do not know how to *genuinely* love those whom we dislike. I believe this is far more true for women than men, and research bears this out.[3]

We need to be mature enough to realize that not everyone will like us. That is probably one of the earliest lessons we learned when we had our first encounter with the little girl who would not play with us on the school playground, as desperately as we tried to win her affection. We should also learn to love ourselves enough and develop our confidence so that we are unaffected by those who, for their own reasons, choose to reject us.

There may be a woman with whom you fellowship within the church setting who has not been insulting to you, nor you to her, but there

---

3. Edwards and Mathews, 95-97.

is an unspoken understanding between the two of you that assures that you do not spend your Saturday afternoons together. This is acceptable, as long as you can wish her well and love her enough to treat her with genuine respect, and you do not intentionally cause tension between the two of you. Thus, my reaction to my former advisor's behavior had nothing to do with her personal dislike for me, but everything to do with her treating me unprofessionally and abandoning her responsibility.

When you are honestly trying to grow up spiritually and you want to make a decision to love your sister, you should welcome at least some opportunities to work with her. Perhaps you will get to know her better. Maybe you will have an opportunity to try to understand what is making her speak or act the way she does. Or maybe you will not, but the prayer and humility that must cover your shared project will open your heart and nurture that love. This is love *in action.*

Too often, I have heard women grudgingly concede, "Okay, I love her, but I don't like her." But they do not do the work of treating that sister with genuine love; they barely tolerate her presence or try to ignore her. When Paul urges us to walk in love, unity, and peace, he does not have mere tolerance in mind, nor is he suggesting that you constantly put distance between the two of you. Such a notion is simply not implied in the qualities that are identified in that Colossians passage, and it could not possibly demonstrate the way you love yourself or the way you would want to be treated.

Everyone will not like us, any more than we will like everyone with whom we have contact, whether it is at church, in our families, or in our places of employment. Still, we are commanded to love them. This means we treat those annoying folks like Jesus would treat them. We honor them, serve them, and find a way to see the image of God in them.

It is difficult to love women who have wounded us, but difficulty does not remove our obligation. We are *commanded* to love because loving the unlovable is unnatural.[4] To do so requires a decision, not a feeling. The world is sensuous, which means worldly people are driven by and operate according to their senses—what they can see, hear, taste, etc. Their desire is to find pleasure through their senses and exclude anything that is contrary to their pleasure seeking. Something about Christian love must look and sound different from the world around us in order for people to be able to identify us according

---

4. Jimmie D. Compton, Jr., "Command to Love One Another," *Hope Bible Fellowship Church's Ministry of the Word.* http://dl.dropbox. com/u/16111363/JComptonJr_ Sermons/AA_Message_Directory.htm (accessed December 28, 2010).

to the badge of love that Jesus told us to wear. We are required to respond to a command by making a decision, not according to how we feel or whether or not we "want to."

We all stumble from time to time. If salvation meant that we would no longer be tempted by sin, we would not need Holy Spirit empowerment. But the Holy Spirit dwells within us to empower us to obey God. He gives us the desire and the power to do the unnatural, such as loving those we dislike and obeying Him when our flesh, the world, and the devil would tempt us to do otherwise. We sometimes give in to our flesh and our own desires and surrender in our battles with the devil because sin is a powerful temptation for *everyone*. But Scripture tells us that "the one who is in you is greater than the one who is in the world" (1 John 4:4).

God has taken into consideration all of the "good reasons" we have for disliking a sister. Her behavior is far more offensive to the holy and perfect God than it is to us, since we are sinful ourselves. Yet, He loves her anyway. How can we do less? In 1 Peter 4:8, He encourages us with these words:

8 Above all, [agapē] each other deeply, because [agapē] covers over a multitude of sins.

I said quite a bit about conflict in Chapter 4. It was important at that point to define what is meant by conflict so we could follow what that demands of leadership. I may have referred to the conflicts as *disputes, disagreements, issues,* or *discord.* But when we look at this matter of the way women treat one another through the lens of the love command, do you see what I see? That is, very often there is no disagreement in opinion or purpose; no open dispute, conflict or even a reasonable basis for opposition; there are no frustrated goals. There is simply the failure to love—to *agapē* one another despite our flaws.

~

Jesus, You have commanded Your daughters to love one another just as You have loved us. You know our weaknesses, so You have given us the power of the indwelling Holy Spirit to shape us into Your likeness. I want to love others the way You love me, Jesus. Some of the women I need to grow to love have hurt me and others and I may feel that they are not worthy of my love, but I am not worthy of Yours. So I ask You, Jesus, to remove any bitterness or hostility that separates us and to place Your will above mine. I ask You to convict me if I have refused to admit any unloving attitude or behavior toward my sisters. If I am harboring feelings of jealousy or ill-will or anything that is so ugly that I cannot admit it to myself, show it to me, Jesus; help me to examine my heart. You alone know me. I submit my heart, my will, and my relationships to You. In Your precious Name, Jesus, grow me up, and help me to become more like You. Amen.

Chapter 7

Heal My Wounded, Broken Spirit!

I stated in the Preface that I am not a counselor and that this book is not meant to be therapeutic. There are many excellent books on emotional healing that would be helpful for those of you whose needs go beyond my purpose (see Recommended Resources following Chapter 8).

Still, I want the Hannahs, Peninnahs, Elkanahs, and Elis to find something here that will minister to the wounds in you and your congregations. While I do not intend to suggest the type of therapy that a professional counselor might in this situation, there are some points that I believe are critical to this discussion and will help you wherever you are in this dilemma. This is not a prioritized list, it is not conclusive, and I do not promise that if you practice all of these principles you will be guaranteed blissful relationships with every woman in your congregation. They are merely suggestions, reminders, and observations that can help you avoid and recover from conflicts that lead to emotional wounds. I hope that you will embrace them in your fellowship.

1. <u>Recognize that help may be needed</u>.

In Matthew 18:15-17, Christ gave the church His guidelines for resolving relationship problems that are caused by sin. We discussed that passage in the chapter on leadership (pp. 50-51). Make every effort to talk to the individual who has wounded you without involving others. Do not be too hasty in seeking outside help. Ask for intervention only if your sister refuses to talk about the matter or if you need encouragement to step up to the challenge. Perhaps you are very timid by nature or the offending individual is another leader—there could be some good reasons for asking for assistance. Pray for the strength that you need to have this difficult conversation. But if you are not making progress and your relationship with her is suffering, it is important to know that you may need help.

I cannot state strongly enough how critical it is that you not allow your incident to become a source of gossip. Know whom you can trust. While you probably have good friends in your congregation, it may be best that you share only with a leader who is a trained or gifted mediator and is able to be objective. If not a leader, your confidante must—absolutely *must*—be a mature Christian who will not become the spark who starts a wildfire of conflict and gossip that will be very difficult to put out. Satan loves this kind of dispute and will have a field day with it if you give him the ammunition.

More than likely, the first question a mediator will ask you is if you have made an attempt to speak with the other individual about the matter. Your having done so is in keeping with biblical guidelines. Think of how you would feel if that sister had been offended by something you said or did, but instead of bringing it to your attention, she shared it with someone else. I have had women try to manipulate me and turn me against other women under the pretense of seeking help for a dispute in which they refused to confront their offender.   That is venomous behavior.

If you honestly believe, even after prayer and self-examination, that you are unable to confront the woman who has hurt you, be certain that the person whose advice you solicit is not just someone who will listen to your side of the story and agree with you. He or she must be qualified to offer godly wisdom and guidance. Hopefully, that person will be able to give you the encouragement you need to have the healing conversation yourself.

Christians sometimes fail to recognize and take advantage of the help that is available to us. We convince ourselves that "All I need to do is pray." Every situation, heartache, or concern we might face should be saturated in prayer. God is able to bring healing through your prayers and the prayers of others. When we read Psalms we see how David and other psalmists took their deepest emotional pain to God, and He lifted them out of despair as they poured their hearts out to Him. Meditate on those Psalms for your own comfort, and also practice other spiritual disciplines such as silence and fasting.[1]

Most of you are probably familiar with the gifts of the Spirit and the ministries that are listed in the letters to the churches.[2] We do ourselves a tremendous disservice by ignoring how God uses these gifts to build up His people. Gifts of helping and guidance are identified in 1 Corinthians 12:28.

> **28** And God has placed in the church first of all apostles, second prophets, third teachers, then miracles, then gifts of healing, of helping, of guidance, and of different kinds of tongues.

---

1. See the Ensley, Foster, and Thompson entries in Recommended Resources, pp. 131-32.
2. Romans 12:4-8; 1 Corinthians 12; Ephesians 4:11; 1 Peter 4:10-11.

Some versions of the Bible call helping and guidance simply "help" or "forms of assistance." Both Paul and Peter emphasize the "different kinds of working" and "various forms" of the gifts and stress that they are *for our good* (1 Corinthians 12:6-7; 1 Peter 4:10). God uses the worship community (the church) to heal His people. Those who are gifted with the ministries of helps and guidance (and of course some other gifts, but these in particular), are often the vessels God chooses to send a word of healing for our wounds.

Gifted members of the church who are not necessarily leaders can be instrumental in encouraging you to face your situation without you bringing them into the matter in a way that requires their direct intervention and without confidentiality being violated. Or perhaps you have a prayer partner whom you know you can trust. Once you have prayed and asked God to reveal the individual you should seek advice from, your conversation might begin with,

I have a situation that I need to address, but I find it very difficult to bring it up. Will you pray for me to be able to speak up and for the matter to be resolved?

It should be just that simple. That individual, if her intentions are honorable and if she is being Spirit led, will not probe for more information. Do not be tempted to offer any, and be careful about what you reveal in your praise reports.

God uses whomever He pleases to bless His children. Think of the Old Testament biblical narrative in which the Israelites were just about to go into the Promised Land, and Joshua sent two spies into Jericho to spy out the land. The king would have had these spies killed if it had not been for Rahab. Yet, even when her name is mentioned in the New Testament nearly fifteen hundred years later, she is still referred to as "Rahab the prostitute."[3] No matter how she was regarded throughout history, though, she was God's chosen vessel to bless His people, and she is named in the ancestry of Christ Himself.

Many years back in my own life, I was in a very difficult place financially. God used a man—a casual acquaintance—who led the most depraved lifestyle, to make opportunities available to me that turned my situation around. This is favor, and God is no less gracious in bestowing it for emotional healing than He is in financial upheaval or other battles in which we are engaged. These realities remind us that we need to be careful how we treat people and view their circumstances. God had to do a miraculous

---

3. Joshua 2; 6:1-25; Hebrews 11:31; James 2:25.

work in every one of us to get us where we are, and we remain his unfinished business.

We live in a sin-sick world. We face opposition daily, and our faith is tested in our trials. When understanding or recovery does not come immediately, we may beat ourselves up and assume we do not have enough faith or that something is wrong with us. We sometimes question God's love for us or His concern about our problem. We languish in depression and anxiety, challenge Him to a miracle of healing, and confuse testing Him, which Scripture forbids, with faith.[4] I believe without question that God performs miracles today. However, I also believe that His promises concerning them are not fully understood and are often mistaught.

Testing God is defiant. It is what happens when you insist that you are waiting for a miracle rather than seeking help, when the truth is that you believe that He should prove Himself by performing one. A test dares Him to do (or not do) something, very much like Satan's challenge (dare) to Jesus in the desert. Not seeking needed help is a matter of fear, laziness, pride, or priorities. Faith, on the other hand, requires a risk. It considers God's Word and submits to His "bigness" and sovereignty to heal you or move in your circumstances in any way He chooses. Let

---

4. Matthew 4:1-7; Psalm 26:2-3; 78:18-22.

God test your faith in Him; by no means are we to test Him as a demand that He prove His character or power.

No matter what situation we face, God, in His infinite love, has provided many avenues of help. Even when emotional wounding is not severe, we may be in a state of confusion as to what we should do in any given situation that is new or challenging. It is appallingly arrogant to presume that you alone will always have the best solution for every dilemma you will ever face. It is also self-defeating, as you may miss out on the benefits of wise, Spirit-led counsel when you ignore the power and gifting of people God has called and sent to help.

Sometimes Christians are reluctant to ask for help in matters related to our mental or spiritual health because we believe that to do so contradicts our faith. We do not want to admit to others or even to ourselves that we need help. We fake it a lot in church. Pride is one of the most rampant, destructive, and easily masked sins in our congregations. It often masquerades as perfectionism, confidence, and other characteristics that we are tempted to admire because those are positive qualities when they are properly nurtured and balanced. However, when pride is an issue, the devil uses our pretense of having it all together to prevent healing for the brokenness that either leads to or results from a Peninnah spirit. Don't let it keep you from seeking help from others.

I urge you to reconsider your decision to just ignore pain or anger that has lingered for some time. Wounds that cause broken fellowship between you and God or you and your sisters should not be ignored just because you have not found a way to address them effectively. God has provided help, and He wants you to use it to repair the brokenness that grips you.

2. <u>Do not rely on the passage of time alone to resolve issues</u>.

Time heals many wounds, but it does not heal *all* wounds, and it allows many of them to fester and grow. Christian clinical psychologist David G. Benner puts it this way:

> The reality is that time is necessary but not sufficient in the healing process. Healing takes time but it also requires much more of an active response on the part of the one who is hurting. When we count on time to produce healing, what we receive is not genuine healing but rather the elimination of feelings through repression, denial, or some other mental mechanism of defense.[5]

---

5. David G. Benner, *Healing Emotional Wounds* (Grand Rapids, MI: Baker Book House, 1990), 52.

Relying on time alone allows you to disregard your responsibility to hold others accountable and restore loving relationships. You should not presume that over time your pain will automatically vanish and that your relationship will be restored without your taking active steps to get it to that point. And what about the relationship in the meantime? Will you fake it for one year, five years, twenty years or more, pretending that nothing is wrong while you wait for that magic day that you wake up and everything is fine? That is not likely to happen.

Perhaps you believe the hurt will subside over time. It will, to a degree, but you are far more likely to have lingering issues and doubts and have a less than genuine relationship with the offender. Saying nothing may feel like an easier choice at the time, but it will probably prove to be the fruitless way out.

Some of you may be reflecting on a wound that is years, even decades old. Should the perpetrator still be confronted if you have not healed from it? First, let me remind you that we are not talking about matters such as incest or other forms of abuse that cause *deep* wounds and psychological harm. For those offenses you need professional guidance. In the matters we are discussing here, it depends.

In addition to the possible conditions on page 75, you would need to consider that individual's present circumstances as well as your own. Perhaps you should bring the issue out into the open if the incident was significant enough to have damaged your relationship and if your motives are pure: healing, love, accountability, and restoration. A troubled relationship can undergo a wonderful renewal by one courageous, prayerful sister airing a matter that has interfered with honest fellowship for many years.

Or perhaps this is a time for you to *really* take it on the chin. Maybe one of those conditions (p. 75) did not apply when the incident occurred, but it does now. It could be that now you really do need to let it go. The maturity required to rise above certain offenses and the prayerfulness and discipline that you need to practice in order to do so are in the interest of your own spiritual and emotional growth. Consider your relationship with that person apart from that offense. Is it fair to hold her to one error if she has otherwise been loving and supportive and you have enjoyed honest fellowship with her? If it is best to leave the matter unaddressed, it remains your responsibility to do so without complaining, self-pity, gossip, vindictiveness, or martyrdom. This is where forgiveness and love must rule.[6]

The difficulty of the decision you have to make is a good reason for dealing with uncomfortable matters when they occur. Years later,

---

6. See the Smedes entry in Recommended Resources, pp. 131-32.

time may not have healed your wound, you may be wrestling with whether or not to bring it up, others may have been hurt because you did not point out the offender's fault, and you will quite possibly be met with a "Why is she dragging this stuff up *now*?" attitude from her. That is a legitimate question that you should be prepared for by answering it first in your own heart.

Do not trivialize the matter of emotional wounding between women. Those minor aggravations should be recognized for what they are, but they can cause painful wounds if they are not dealt with. Pain turns to anger, and anger can easily become bitterness if it is not expressed in a healthy way.

3. <u>Do not allow a reprimand or difference in opinions to be taken as personal rejection.</u>

This speaks to an interesting reality in women's conflicts. Satan rears his ugly head and twists a needed word of correction or a harmless opinion into what is mistaken for a personal attack. Women's differences about a spiritual or biblical matter can quickly escalate and become personal.[7] This is made even worse when they find it difficult to be honest about their feelings. When men disagree, they disagree about an is-

---

7. Edwards and Mathews, 154.

sue without that disagreement affecting how they relate to one another. The same is generally not true for women, but we can recognize that hindrance and overcome it.

Like most of you, I have been in meetings or classes with groups of women in which issues were being discussed and opinions expressed. If there was strong disagreement—no matter how impersonal—tension often arose that lingered long after the meeting was over. Disagreeing with a sister about the theme for this year's Vacation Bible School or the meaning of a passage of Scripture should not have any impact on your personal relationship. Neither of you should leave the meeting with any feelings of anger, hurt, or annoyance. If you have the slightest notion that the other individual has any of those feelings, it would be easier to resolve the matter at that moment than it will be for you to bring it up later, after either of you has allowed what should have been a meaningless difference in opinions to change the way the two of you relate.

An excellent example of this principle is illustrated in Jesus' relationships with His disciples. He chastised them several times, publicly and sternly.

In Matthew 16:23 we read:

23 Jesus turned and said to Peter, "Get behind me, Satan! You are a stumbling block to me; you do not have in mind the things of God, but the things of men."

Jesus reprimanded Peter for his moment of ungodly thinking, but earlier in that same passage (vv. 13-20), we read that Jesus had blessed Peter for recognizing that He was God his Savior. It was the truth of their relationship that humbled Peter following his denial of Christ so that he could be restored to Him (Matthew 26:31-75).

In Matthew 17:17-20 we see Christ chastising His disciples again:

> **17** "O unbelieving and perverse generation," Jesus replied, "how long shall I stay with you? How long shall I put up with you? . . ."
> **19** Then the disciples came to Jesus in private and asked, "Why couldn't we drive [the demon] out?"
> **20** He replied, "Because you have so little faith. . . ."

Despite having been publicly corrected, how did John see himself in relationship to Jesus? Throughout his Gospel, John refers to himself as "the disciple whom Jesus loved" (John 13:23; 19:26; 20:2; 21:7; 21:20). John placed more emphasis on love and used the term far more than any of the other Gospel writers. He, along with his brother James and Peter, had a closer, more intimate relationship with Jesus than any of the other disciples. John knew this, embraced it, and did not allow that truth to be threatened by the occasions that Jesus needed to speak sternly to their human flaws.

It was not only that Jesus loved his disciples, but that they walked in the *truth* of His love in their relationship with Him, despite having been chastised. They did not operate in their feelings; they operated in truth. This is what we must learn to do with God and with our sisters.

4. <u>Stop emotional wounding before it begins</u>.

When my mother was in rehabilitation following back surgery several years ago, she went through some periods of intense pain. She has always been an avid reader, and she closely follows news stories concerning health and medical issues. She has a healthy awareness of prescription drug addiction, and despite the agonizing pain from the condition that led to her surgery, she was often reluctant to take medication. Even in that controlled medical environment following her surgery, she would only accept medication when the pain became unbearable. By then, her nurses told her, it was more difficult to manage. They had to tell her repeatedly, "Get in front of the pain." In other words, the pain was much more difficult to manage once it started.

It is easier to prevent strife than it is to repair it. Healing is not a matter of pretending that you love someone or maintaining a sham of a relationship; it is retraining your thoughts about that individual. Your heart may need to be purged of old feelings so that *agapē* rules and guides you. Internalize the principles of love and peace that we are taught in Scripture, and allow the Holy Spirit to change you. Those principles will shape your behavior and guard your heart and your tongue in relationships. You will not just *do* those loving acts, but you will *become* a more loving individual. God has made it clear that this is His will for us.

In *A Tale of Three Kings*, author Gene Edwards discusses "Christian clashes" based on the biblical account of Saul, David, and Absalom as it is told in 1 and 2 Samuel. He discusses those clashes in terms of what he calls "spear throwing." Whatever your role is in your church, it could be very helpful for you to commit to the principles Edwards suggests. They can teach a great deal about preventing conflicts before they start.

Edwards begins,

You can easily tell when someone has been hit by a spear. [She] turns a deep shade of bitter.[8]

Scripture uses the term *bitterness* to describe a wicked, scandalous person or a dangerous sin that could lead to backsliding (Hebrews 12:15). Emotional wounds can lead to bitterness. God

---

8. Taken from *A Tale of Three Kings* by Gene Edwards. Copyright © 1980 by Gene Edwards. Used by permission of Tyndale House Publishers, Inc. All rights reserved. 19-20.

never tells us not to *be* angry, but to *manage* our anger. However, we are told to rid ourselves of *all* bitterness (James 1:19; Ephesians 4:26, 31).

Bitterness is defined as a prolonged, resentful feeling of being disempowered, devalued, and victimized. It results from the long-term mismanagement of annoyance, irritation, frustration, anger, or rage.[9] Therefore, the "ordinary pain" that causes emotional wounds may be minor annoyances, but they can lead to anger and bitterness if they are not properly managed.

One factor in managing anger is facing the issue in a constructive way. Following my encounter with the woman in that leadership class (pp. 25-26), I allowed my humiliation to bully me into silence. The decision not to confront a Peninnah is only valid if we make the decision to move past the incident in an honest, spiritually and emotionally healthy way. Anger results from hurts that we experience, but I praise God that He did not allow me to wallow in my hurt feelings and nurse them into bitterness. It was to my advantage to stop brooding and feeling anger toward someone who was not present and who

---

9. Stephen Diamond, "Anger Disorder (Part Two): Can Bitterness Become a Mental Disorder?" *Pschologytoday. com*, June 3, 2009, under "Evil Deeds: A Forensic Psychologist on Anger, Madness and Destructive Behavior," http://www.psychologytoday.com/blog/evil-deeds (accessed December 20, 2010).

never had a significant role in my life. Through prayer and meditation on the Word, I moved from being humiliated and angry to refusing to let the devil have that victory in my thought life.

Edwards goes on to share three things that David had apparently learned that kept him from being hit by the spears that were being launched at him. These principles are brief and can easily be rehearsed and called upon in the times that you are challenged. Better yet, they can become so deeply a part of you that they rule your relationships. I believe I can add some insight to each of those warnings:

One, never learn anything about the fashionable, easily mastered art of spear throwing.[10]

Most of us have been both Hannah and Peninnah. It is my prayer that as we grow and recognize the damage we are doing to our sisters and the church and learn to walk in true love, we will see less of Peninnah in ourselves.

It is very rare to encounter anyone who does not have a few spears ready to launch. One of my most treasured friends, Pat, was a woman I never heard say anything negative about anyone. When I sat with mutual friends sharing

10. Edwards, 19-20.

memories of her following her passing in 2007, one person after another voiced the same "criticism" I had lovingly teased Pat about from time to time: "She was too nice."

On some level, that may be a legitimate concern for some individuals. But my point is that I honestly believe that Pat knew nothing about spear throwing. More likely, it was through her own experiences of being the target of so much criticism that she chose not to be guilty of it herself. So it is possible to overcome this behavior. Although it has already been learned and is practiced too often by so many of us, we can resolve to cover it with love so that it becomes as ugly to us as it is to Christ. It is a habit for some that needs to be replaced by a different habit.

Edwards continues,

Two, stay out of the company of all spear throwers.[11]

Are there spear throwers in your congregation? Do not take on a superior position, and do not indulge in behavior that would cause division, but perhaps you can influence those agitators. Talk honestly with a sister if she wounds you, and refuse to stand by and listen when she wounds others. At that point, you become in-

---

11. Ibid.

strumental in her growth and you are protecting your own spiritual and emotional health.

As Edwards stated, spear throwing is an easily mastered art. When you are in the company of those who habitually wound others with their mouths through gossip, slander, and snide comments, it becomes too easy to join in with them and begin throwing your own spears. Apostle Paul had no problem with warning us about our associations. His admonition that "Bad company corrupts good character" (1 Corinthians 15:33) should be taken as truth inside and outside of the church. But remember that the goal was always restoration, and that must be our mindset.

Edwards then states,

And three, keep your mouth tightly closed.[12]

This warning has to do with gossip and complaining; it does not suggest that the perpetrator should not be confronted in an effort to solve the problem. The "silence" that surrounds emotional wounding does not mean that victims are actually keeping silent about hurt feelings and conflicts. They are talking about their wounds, but not in a way that would bring healing.

---

12. Ibid.

We do far too much "sharing" of sensitive matters under the pretense of seeking advice, requesting prayer, or voicing concern. It is nothing more than gossip and a despicable, *perhaps subconscious* attempt to smear a sister's character. Except for the purpose of mediation, sharing an offense with mutual acquaintances serves *no* purpose other than to belittle that person in the eyes of others. Avoid this temptation. Having sought one person's advice or confidence, how many more people have you shared the offense with? Is it simply being repeated until you find someone who agrees with your position? Repentance may be in order.

Gossip is a very destructive habit that women often participate in within the church. I realize that some men gossip too, and sometimes more than women. However, gossip is almost never the source of their conflicts. It is not harmless or insignificant to God. When Paul talks about lawlessness and sinfulness in Romans 1:18-32, he includes gossip in that list of sins. He cautions against it in 1 Timothy 5:13, as well.

Conflicts become far more difficult to resolve when you bring people into the discussion who are not directly involved, either as part of the conflict itself, or to mediate, if necessary. You will have allowed them to form and share their opinions, take sides, and pass judgment without their having the benefit of hearing both sides of the matter. There is nothing constructive in this repeated sharing. Has someone's character been damaged because of your one-sided reporting of an event? How will you salvage her reputation when the two of you are able to put that dispute behind you and move on in genuine love and fellowship? (It will be your responsibility to do so!) When healing occurs, you will then have to change the thinking of more people, which may not be possible. The fire will have spread by then.

Edwards concludes with this regarding his three cautions:

> In this way, spears will never touch you, even when they pierce your heart. [13]

You may be in Hannah's position temporarily, but God loves you and wants you to be whole. As you grow, you can learn to dodge those spears as skillfully as David. Even when you are wounded, those spears do not have to touch or change who you are fundamentally. They hurt, but they should not negatively change your character, or, although it may be difficult, the way you respond to the spear thrower. They certainly should not change the way you relate to other individuals or your healthy knowledge of who you are as a person. Remember the love

---

13. Ibid.

principles and especially the warning against returning evil for evil (Romans 12:17-21). It is better to use the "hurt people hurt people" theory as a warning than as an excuse.

5. <u>Pray for the individual who has wounded you or someone else.</u>

This might be difficult at first, but do not let that stop you. Keep at it, knowing that this is God's will and that He is in there with you. When I have a difficult relationship with *anyone*, whether it is a sister in Christ or an unsaved co-worker, I pray for her. Not the "Oh Lord, please see fit to help her find another church," or "Please let her stay home from work tomorrow" type of prayer; but truly lifting her up, praying for her needs, and praying for the pain in her life that may be causing her to act out toward me or others. Praying for her gives power to your decision to love her and see her as God sees her—through the lens of Christ.

In Romans 12:12-16, Paul had congregational relationships in mind when he wrote,

12 Be joyful in hope, patient in affliction, faithful in prayer.
13 Share with the Lord's people who are in need. Practice hospitality.
14 Bless those who persecute you; bless and do not curse.
15 Rejoice with those who rejoice; mourn with those who mourn.

¹⁶ Live in harmony with one another. Do not be proud, but be willing to associate with people of low position. Do not be conceited.

These commands are the opposites of some of the causes and effects of emotional wounding. Patience despite affliction is directly opposed to the annoyance that would lead to wounding others or the agitation we might experience as a response to those annoyances. Rejoicing with those who rejoice puts jealousy to flight. Associating with those of low position builds bridges over the divisions that sometimes exist between the people of God; it comes against arrogance and conceit.

The affliction that has been imposed on you is an opportunity for you to pray for your sister. You need to do this because of your love for Christ and in obedience to His Word. It is as much for your own sake as hers. It is fine if you have to pray for the desire to pray for her first. There is nothing wrong with having to pray yourself into God's will. Many of my prayers begin with confession about what is in my heart about someone that I know should not be there. God already knows—He is waiting for us to be honest with Him.

Your prayer may be much like the prayer we prayed for Peninnah in Chapter 2. For example,

Father, I lift up my sister _____ before You now. I thank You that because of the

blood of Jesus, we have a relationship with You, and we have a relationship with one another. You know the conflict between us, Father, and I know that the resentment and bitterness in my heart are not pleasing to You. We are Your daughters, You love us both, and You would have us to live in peace with one another and to love one another. I am hurt, God. I want to love _____, but because of my pain, I know I cannot do this without You. You know her, and You know her pain. You know what causes her to lash out at others. You know her needs and her concerns. So I ask You now, Father, to minister to _____'s needs. Only You know her heart, so I ask You to speak into the empty and hurting places and help her to feel Your love and Your presence. Help others and me to be patient with _____, just as You have been patient with us. . . .

You get the idea. It is impossible to continue to feel hostility toward someone when you honestly open your heart to pray for her. It may not happen right away, and you should pray for her on a regular basis. What you have to ask yourself is if you really want your relationship to be mended. It requires honesty with yourself to admit that you are not yet in the place where you desire reconciliation.

Chapter 8

The Gates of Hell

The church existed in the mind of Christ before the day of Pentecost. Before He told Peter, "Upon this rock I will build my church," before the disciples were sent out to evangelize the world, and before Apostle Paul set about his first journey, Jesus already knew the church as a body of believers—not a building with stained glass and four walls as we tend to think of it today.

The church as an institution may have been birthed at Pentecost (Acts 2), but Jesus is not making up His plan for humanity as He goes along. He knew before it was born what it would look like when He returns for it. Since He knew the end at the beginning, there are two things that we should keep in mind concerning the matter of relationships between women in the church:

1. Jesus knew that the church would face challenges from the inside as well as the outside.
2. Jesus knew what He intended the church to be.

The very last prayer that Jesus uttered on earth was for unity among believers (John 16). His expectation was that we would be one, just as He is one with the Father. This means, for example, that believers in the United States are one, because we share in the same Spirit with believers in every part of the world. It means that First Baptist should be able to fellowship with Second Presbyterian. And it also means that women should be able to dwell peacefully and lovingly with one another.

Scripture has not ignored the reality of the tension and conflict that may arise among believers. Virtually every one of the epistles cautions us to live in harmony with one another (Romans 15:5-7; 1 Corinthians 1:10; 2 Corinthians 13:11; Galatians 5:19-22; Ephesians 4:3; Philippians 2:3; Colossians 3:13; 1 Thessalonians 5:13-15; and so on). Similarly, every book of the Bible recounts cases of conflict and division between the people of God.

In Ephesians 4:3 where Paul warns, "Make every effort to keep the unity of the Spirit through the bond of peace," the phrase *make every effort* is translated from the Greek word *spoudazo* and means that one must agonize and strive for this peace as a gladiator would have fought to the death in the Coliseum.[1] None of us should expect to participate in the family of God free from the friction that naturally occurs when diverse personalities meet. Remember, unity does not mean uniformity. But we should be prepared to respond to that friction in love and with a desire for oneness and peace. Jesus was prepared for even the gates of hell.

The church is not perfect. Do not think that Christ's return for a church "without stain or wrinkle" (Ephesians 5:27) means that it must be. The church is not holy because of the people who comprise it; the church is holy because Christ is holy, and the church is founded on Him. It is His body, from which He is inseparable. Jesus sacrificed Himself for the church for His own purposes (Ephesians 5:25-27; Colossians 1:18-19). That sacrifice was perfect and blameless, and through over two thousand years of conflict, scandal, and yes, even women who are not always nice to each other, that perfect sacrifice is sufficient to hold back even the gates of Hell until He returns.

Jesus loves His church. Despite our imperfections, as sociologist and pastor Dr. Tony Campolo observes, "We are still God's best

---

1. Sande, 52.

chance at showcasing what the whole world will become when the kingdom of God becomes fully actualized."[2]

We should do our best to represent Him well.

---

2. Brian D. McLaren and Tony Campolo, *Adventures in Missing the Point: How the Culture-controlled Church Neutered the Gospel* (Grand Rapids, MI: Zondervan, 2003), 55. Copyright © 2003 by Brian D. McLaren and Tony Campolo. Used by permission of Zondervan, www.zondervan.com.

We probably all see ourselves somewhere in this story, if not as Hannah or Peninnah, then perhaps as Elkanah or Eli. You have your own stories. I have my own, and I have heard far too many others. I can testify to God's power to heal our pain and anger. Wherever we find Peninnah's agitation in the church, we will also find Hannahs who are wounded and weary. Christ is there with them, preparing His bride, the church, for His return. She is the bride for which He sacrificed Himself, and He loves her despite her flaws. His Word and His virtues bring healing into the places of her deepest wounds.

Despite any amount of pain that we endure on this side of glory, it does not equal the joy we will experience for eternity. Meanwhile, is it fair for Hannah to be victimized, even if Peninnah is hurting? Jesus Christ is perfect and sinless, yet

He died on the cross for my sins; therefore, I will refrain from making judgments that suit me solely on the basis of "fairness."

I would like to ask that we all, including myself, do something. That is, re-read this book in another year or two. Commit to revisiting these principles regularly. The Scriptures on which this book is based are fundamental to our Christian fellowship. But we need to go back to those foundational teachings from time to time. Let's examine ourselves periodically and see if damaged relationships have been mended, if we have done a better job of guarding our tongues, and if we are, indeed, loving our sisters as we love ourselves.

We are obligated to change wounding behavior. I truly believe that we want to stop the pain and anger, whether we are Hannah, Peninnah, Elkanah, or Eli. The silence surrounding women's mistreatment of one another does not hide the reality of the woundedness we have inflicted on our sisters by failing to *really* love them—just as Jesus loves us.

Recommended Resources

Burchett, Dave. *When Bad Christians Happen to Good People: Where We Have Failed Each Other and How to Reverse the Damage.* Colorado Springs, CO: Waterbrook Press, 2002.

Compton, Jimmie D., Jr. "Loving One Another: The 2nd Greatest Command." *Hope Bible Fellowship Church's Ministry of the Word.* http://dl.dropbox.com/u/16111363/JCo mptonJr_Sermons/AA_Message_Directory. htm.

Ensley, Eddie. *Prayer That Heals Our Emotions.* San Francisco: Harper & Row Publishers, 1986.

Foster, Richard J. *Celebration of Discipline: The Path to Spiritual Growth.* San Francisco: HarperSanFrancisco, 1998.

Frank, Jan. *Door of Hope: Recognizing and Resolving the Pains of Your Past.* Nashville, TN: Thomas Nelson Publishers, 1995.

131

Mansfield, Stephen. *ReChurch: Healing Your Way Back to the People of God.* Carol Stream, IL: BarnaBooks, 2010.

Murren, Doug. *Churches That Heal: Becoming a Church That Mends Broken Hearts and Restores Shattered Lives.* West Monroe, LA: Howard Publishing Co., 1999.

Smedes, Lewis B. *Forgive and Forget: Healing the Hurts We Don't Deserve.* New York: HarperCollins, 1996.

Thompson, Marjorie. *Soul Feast: An Invitation to the Christian Spiritual Life.* Louisville, KY: Westminster John Knox Press, 1995.

Wardle, Terry. *Healing Care Healing Prayer: Helping the Broken Find Wholeness in Christ.* Abilene, TX: Leafwood Publishers, 2001.

_____. *Outrageous Love Transforming Power: How the Holy Spirit Shapes You into the Likeness of Christ.* Abilene, TX: Leafwood Publishers, 2004.

_____. *Wounded: How to Find Wholeness and Inner Healing in Christ.* Abilene, TX: Leafwood Publishers, 2005.

Wilson, Sandra D. *Hurt People Hurt People: Hope and Healing for Yourself and Your Relationships.* Grand Rapids, MI: Discovery House Publishers, 2001.

Bibliography

Benner, David G. *Healing Emotional Wounds.*
Grand Rapids, MI: Baker Book House,
1990.

Bergen, Robert D. *The New American
Commentary.* Nashville, TN: B & H
Publishing Group, 1996.

Compton, Jimmie D., Jr. "Command to Love One
Another." *Hope Bible Fellowship Church's
Ministry of the Word.* http://dl.dropbox.
com/u/16111363/JComptonJr_Sermons/
AA_Message_Directory.htm (accessed
December 28, 2010).

Crabb, Larry. *The Safest Place on Earth: Where
People Connect and Are Forever Changed.*
Nashville, TN: W Publishing Group, 1999.

Diamond, Stephen. "Anger Disorder (Part Two):
Can Bitterness Become a Mental
Disorder?" *Pschologytoday.com.* http://
www.psychology today.com/blog/evil-

deeds/ 200906/anger-disorder-part-two-can-bitterness-become-mental-disorder (accessed December 20, 2010).

Edwards, Gene. *A Tale of Three Kings: A Study in Brokenness.* Carol Stream, IL: Tyndale House Publishers, Inc., 1992.

Edwards, Sue, and Kelley Mathews. *Leading Women Who Wound: Strategies for an Effective Ministry.* Chicago: Moody Publishers, 2009.

Evans, Mary J. *1 and 2 Samuel.* New International Biblical Commentary. Old Testament Series. Peabody, MA: Hendrickson Publishers, 2000.

Evans, Tony. *Time to Get Serious: Daily Devotions to Keep You Close to God.* Wheaton, IL: Crossway Books, 1995.

Firth, David G. *1 and 2 Samuel.* Apollos Old Testament Commentary. Nottingham, England: Apollos, 2009.

Keil, C.F. and F. Delitzsch. *Joshua, Judges, Ruth, 1 and 2 Samuel.* Vol. 2 of *Commentary on the Old Testament.* Peabody, MA: Hendrickson Publishers, Inc., 2006.

Klein, Ralph W. *First Samuel.* Word Biblical Commentary 10. Waco, TX: Word Books, 1982.

McLaren, Brian D., and Tony Campolo. *Adventures in Missing the Point: How the Culture-controlled Church Neutered the Gospel.* Grand Rapids, MI: Zondervan, 2003.

Sande, Ken. *The Peacemaker: A Biblical Guide to Resolving Personal Conflict.* Grand Rapids, MI: Baker Books, 2004.

Wardle, Terry. *Healing Care Healing Prayer: Helping the Broken Find Wholeness in Christ.* Abilene, TX: Leafwood Publishers, 2001.

_____. *Outrageous Love Transforming Power: How the Holy Spirit Shapes You into the Likeness of Christ.* Abilene, TX: Leafwood Publishers, 2004.

Wilson, Sandra D. *Hurt People Hurt People: Hope and Healing for Yourself and Your Relationships.* Grand Rapids, MI: Discovery House Publishers, 2001.